SpringerBriefs in Electrical and Computer Engineering

For further volumes:
http://www.springer.com/series/10059

Tonghua Su

Chinese Handwriting Recognition: An Algorithmic Perspective

 Springer

Dr. Tonghua Su
School of Software/School of Computer
    Science and Technology
Harbin Institute of Technology
Harbin
Heilongjiang
People's Republic of China

ISSN 2191-8112   ISSN 2191-8120   (electronic)
ISBN 978-3-642-31811-5   ISBN 978-3-642-31812-2   (eBook)
DOI 10.1007/978-3-642-31812-2
Springer Heidelberg New York Dordrecht London

Library of Congress Control Number: 2012955476

Printed on acid-free paper

Springer is part of Springer Science+Business Media (www.springer.com)

Foreword

A study on printed Chinese character recognition was first attempted in the mid-1960s in the United States (Casey and Nagy 1966). In the late-1970s a printed Kanji recognition system was built in Japan where Chinese characters are commonly used as Kanji. Around the same time, the Electrotechnical Laboratory in Japan collected and released a hand printed Kanji database ETL-8 to initiate research on hand printed Chinese character recognition. In the 1980s, significant feature extraction and character recognition techniques such as chain code histogram and MQDF were proposed by a group of Mie University and began to be widely employed in Chinese character recognition. Because of the huge requirements on the storage and processing time the research on Chinese character recognition of those days used to be carried out on mainframe computers or more typically on super computers, while commercial OCR systems were implemented employing hardware technologies such as micro programming, DSP, and dedicated LSI.

Great advances had been witnessed in the constrained handwritten Chinese character recognition and the restricted domain during the 1990s. In the 1990s handwritten address recognition techniques were realized based on the integrated segmentation-recognition strategy for automatic mail sorting in the United States and in the late-1990s mail sorting machines based on the similar strategy for handwritten Kanji address were deployed in Japan. With the rapid progress of personal computers the commercial OCR software for Chinese character recognition was released and became widely available in this period. With increasing industrial demands on further performance improvement and more naturally handwritten samples, extension of the recognition target, e.g., unconstrained handwritten Chinese text, has been raised and activated many researches in this area since then to the present.

This book provides an excellent algorithmic perspective of Chinese handwriting recognition. After a thorough survey on the algorithmic development of Chinese character recognition, the details of the large-scale database, HIT-MW, collected by Harbin Institute of Technology are described. The research on unconstrained handwritten Chinese text can be conducted with the support of HIT-MW database. Then, the integrated segmentation-recognition strategy embedded with MQDF classifier is constructed incrementally. In particular, an effective and scalable PL-MQDF is devised. Most of all, the deep investigation on HMM-based segmentation-free strategy for Chinese handwriting recognition should be highlighted. The sophiscated algorithms to improve the performance are of significant inspiration to Markov model-based systems. Although segmentation and recognition are often treated conveniently as two different processes, those in human recognition of characters seem to be more concurrent and simultaneous. From my point of view this book is expected to contribute widely to the progress of this research area in the future.

28 October 2012   Prof. Fumitaka Kimura
                                                                      Graduate School of Engineering
                                                                                     Mie University

Reference

R. Casey, G. Nagy, Recognition of printed Chinese characters. IEEE Trans. Electron. Comput. EC-**15**(1), 91–101 (1966)

Preface

Creating a practical Chinese handwriting recognizer from scratch is no mean feat. First of all, you need to ensure the availability of sufficient handwritten samples and/or have to collect your own. It took my group three entire years to compile the HIT-MW database. The design and implementation involves thorough evaluation of the state-of-the-art algorithms, ranging from image preprocessing and feature extraction to classifier training and path decoding. You also need to balance the efficacy and training workload. Thus, this book is devoted to helping interested researchers/engineers/students quickly embark on their study of Chinese handwriting recognition.

This work also reflects my ten years of experience in Chinese handwriting recognition. First, it presents an overview of Chinese handwriting recognition within the context of the character recognition field, with an emphasis on the algorithmic developments and shifts from standard databases. Considering the huge challenges posed by realistic Chinese handwriting recognition, we had to stand on the shoulders of giants. Two strategies, the segmentation-free and integrated segmentation-recognition strategy, are pursued in the literature. Recent developments in these strategies are investigated and algorithms that have worked well in practice are primarily focused on in this book. In order to provide a concrete and valuable reference resource, all algorithms are tested on standard databases.

The book employs a "simple-to-complex" organizing principle. As such, the division of the chapters is not on the basis of system components, e.g., preprocessing, feature extraction, classifier design, etc. Instead, baseline systems are initially presented and are subsequently expanded on and incrementally improved. For better comprehension, the first chapter provides a bird's-eye view and Chap. 2 presents a dedicated scheme for establishing the HIT-MW database. In this way, readers have the freedom to begin with whichever chapter they prefer.

I owe a considerable debt of gratitude to many people with regard to this book. First and foremost, I want to thank my mentors, Prof. Tianwen Zhang, Prof. Chenglin Liu, and Prof. Huizhi Lv. I could never have done this without their guidance and encouragement. I especially want to acknowledge the support of Prof. Fumitaka

Kimura who contributed the foreword for this book. Kimura's distinguished accomplishments, such as MQDF, have significantly shaped the field of handwritten Chinese character recognition. Special thanks go to Celine Chang and her assistant Jane Li at Springer Asia for their fantastic work in improving this book considerably. I would like to acknowledge my production editor Nithiya Sivaraman at Springer, and Mr. Srinivas and his typesetting team at Scientific Publishing Services, Chennai, India for the production of this book. I am sincerely grateful to Dr. Bin Lin and Dejun Guan for their constant encouragement, valuable feedback, and unconditional support throughout the long years of my academic career. I also want to thank the many colleagues and former students, who contributed their insights and invaluable comments. In pursuing my work, the following funds should be acknowledged: the National Natural Science Foundation of China (Grants no. 60475011, 60933010, 60975020 and 61203260), the Heilongjiang Natural Science Foundation of China (Grant no. F0322), and China Postdoctoral Science Foundation (Grant no. 20090450623). Finally, my special thanks go to my wife Sara Gong for her unfailing love, support, and patience.

31 October 2012   Tonghua Su

Contents

Chapter 1
Introduction

Abstract Chinese character recognition, as an attractive toolset for Chinese digital library projects, has been drawing intense attention. The Chinese character system is used for communication and has served various political purposes in China, having played an important role in the development of Chinese civilization for over 3000 years. Thus, there are a large number of invaluable archives and documents recorded in Chinese, awaiting conversion as readable text for world-wide sharing. As an indispensable branch, Chinese handwriting recognition has been viewed as one of the most difficult pattern recognition tasks that pose its own unique challenges, such as huge variations in strokes, diversity of writing styles, and a large set of confusable categories. With ever-increasing amounts of training data, researchers have been developing effective algorithms to discern characters from different categories and compensate for the sample variations within the same category. With the help of their efforts, substantial achievements have been made in the field of Chinese handwriting recognition. In this book, essential algorithms for effective Chinese handwriting recognition are presented.

1.1 Background

Chinese character input through western keyboard has been a difficult job. This hinders the process of Chinese information processing. The standard keyboard, invented in the West, is ad hoc made for alphanumeric characters. Therefore to enter Chinese characters into computers, scholars have approached it in three different ways. One tries to construct a super-keyboard with a key per character. As each stroke produces a Chinese character, this scheme requires the least key-strokes. For the total number of the characters is huge, the volume and number of buttons is unfortunately large. However, fast hitting the target button precisely is a

T. Su, *Chinese Handwriting Recognition: An Algorithmic Perspective*,
SpringerBriefs in Electrical and Computer Engineering,
DOI: 10.1007/978-3-642-31812-2_1, © The Author(s) 2013

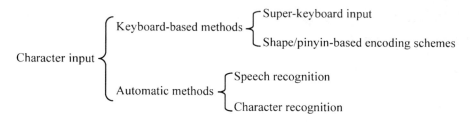

Fig. 1.1 Methods to transcribe Chinese documents

great challenge to the typewriters' intelligent memory and physical strength. Ultimately, it never came to fruition (Fig. 1.1).

Another method depends on character encoding merely through a standard keyboard. Pinyin-based (phonetic) and shape-based are two fundamental encoding schemes. They are usually called "Chinese input methods". Both schemes have their strengths and weaknesses. Shape-based schemes can enter text much faster than pinyin ones, although it takes a longer time to learn. Similarly, Pinyin schemes can be learned much faster at the cost of limited throughput. These schemes are currently prevalent in China, but their intensive human–machine interaction constitutes a heavy burden. A typewriter should exclusively operate on the computer, entering text character by character. Obviously, it is incapable of batch document processing.

For the last method, specialists from pattern recognition field had been devising automatic machines to recognize characters replacing manual keystroke. Speech recognition and character recognition are two main branches. Speech recognition can convert utterances to text and character recognizer reads written text. Both of them aim at mimicking human perception and intelligence, providing a natural human–machine interaction.

1.2 Motivation

The research on character recognition predates the emergence of computer. In 1929, Taushek from Austria filed the first optical character recognition (OCR) patent (Tauschek 1929). The reading machine is built for punch-card accounting using optics and mechanics. The input pattern is projected and matched with predefined mechanical masks. The final decision is issued by a photodetector. Once computer is equipped with researchers as a powerful and convenient facility, OCR can be undertaken and driven widely. Just like the history of artificial intelligence, the difficulties associated with OCR were underestimated by the initial pioneers. They took ideal OCR products for granted in few years. As already known, early researchers were too optimistic. Till the mid 1960s, they realized the difficulty and more investigations were conducted in depth. After a half century's endeavors, considerable advances have been made, stimulating an intelligent society. Meanwhile, more and more challenging problems are distilled from industrial requirements.

For character recognition, there are two acquisition modes, online or offline. In the first case, sensing devices such as tablet or touch screen allow the computer to record the trajectory of the pen tip. In the second case, character patterns may be printed or written on papers. Printed or written documents can be digitized as images through scanners or cameras. The main difference is that online data contains temporal information that is not available in the offline case. Furthermore, character recognition can also be divided into handwriting recognition and printed text recognition. Mature products had been available in printed-form text for decades, while handwriting recognition is still unsolved (Fig. 1.2).

Chinese character recognition has been drawing intense attention as an attractive toolset for Chinese digital library projects. Chinese character system is used for communication and has served various political purposes in China, having played an important role in the development of Chinese civilization over 3000 years. It is now used by one-fourth of the world's population. Thus, there are a large number of invaluable archives and documents recorded in Chinese awaiting conversion as readable text for worldwide sharing. On the other hand, Chinese character recognition has been considered an interesting and intellectually challenging problem in its own right. It comprises a large category symbols and complicated structure. Especially, the handwritten Chinese character recognition is termed as one of the most difficult tasks in pattern recognition due to remarkable writing variabilities. Therefore, advances in Chinese character recognition may indicate great progress of computing intelligence.

Handwritten Chinese character recognition has been studied since the 1980s, Great advances are made, for example, some literatures report recognition rate as high as 99 % (Dai et al. 2007). It is misinterpreted that handwritten Chinese character recognition problem is well solved. The astonishing result only applies to handprinted samples. Whenever a realistic dataset is desired, the results degenerate greatly (Su et al. 2009; Liu 2008). In the recent Chinese character recognition contest, the best recognition rate is no more then 93 % (Liu et al. 2010), concerning 3,755 character classes. Finding out the gaps of the state-of-the-art technology, also reveals the new chances to the researchers in this field. The reasons underlying the gaps mainly result from both the uniqueness of Chinese character (e.g., large amount of classes, complex structure, variable character size, and many similar characters) and diversity of writing style (e.g., different writers, cursive and continuous writing). If the classification algorithm can not simultaneously tolerate

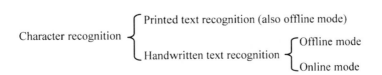

Fig. 1.2 Types of character recognition tasks according to their forms

the variability in same character class and discern the difference between two distinct classes, it is nontrivial to correctly recognize the Chinese character.

An era of handwritten Chinese text recognition has emerged since 2006. As a foundational data, the HIT-MW database (Su et al. 2006) was released in that year. The trend gradually moves from isolated-character recognition to realistic Chinese text. Motivated by the challenging problems provided in (Su 2008; Su et al. 2009), a steady progress can be observed merely in 5 years. First, more unconstrained handwritten text databases are released. Such resources make it possible to design more advanced recognition algorithms. More details will be provided in Sect. 1.3.

Second, different insights are employed to deal with this task and their evolvement has improved recognition rates while reducing the running costs. Generally, the recognition framework can be classified as segmentation-free framework based on probabilistic graphical model and integrated segmentation-recognition framework. These are discussed in Chaps. 3, 4, 5.

Third, we report the recognition results on HIT-MW database. In 2008, the recognition correct rate is about 53.35 % when limited training samples are used. (Su 2008); incorporating a bigram constraint and using a set of synthetic samples, the recognition rate is increased to 73.89 % (Su and Liu 2010). In 2009, a recognition rate of 78.44 % is reported (Wang et al. 2009). A slight improvement in recognition rate is witnessed in 2010 (Li 2010). More recently, a meticulous recognizer can yield a recognition rate as high as over 90 % (Wang et al. 2012b). Surely, steady advances can be observed in the recognition task of handwritten Chinese text. However, even to the advanced recognizers, there are urgent request for a thorough investigation.

1.3 Chronological Survey

It is nearly half a century since the inception of Chinese character recognition. The substantial evolvement can be broken down into five periods. In each period, we will track the origin and following development of the popular algorithms that have been served as the-state-of-the art; describe the shift of research scope from ease to next order of difficulty and discuss the standard character databases supporting the algorithmic development.

1.3.1 Infant Period (~1970)

The early works in this period manifest that the difficulties were harsher than what people expected. The earliest study problem was how to recognize printed numeric. In 1954, Rohland presented his system. Next, the research scope extended to printed alphanumeric (Rohland 1956). In 1958, Electrotechnical Laboratory (ETL) in Japan released a system tackling the printed alphanumeric of

72 classes (Iijima et al. 1963). Some commercial products appeared to deal with printed letters of dedicated specification around 1962. For example, IBM1418 only processes the IBM407 font (Greanias 1962). In this period, two standard hand-printed alphanumeric databases, named Highleyman (Highleyman 1961) and Munson (Munson 1968) respectively, were made publicly available. The recognition scope expanded to the handprinted alphanumeric. The significant role of standard character samples was recognized.

In this period, substantial theoretical foundations had been established. The statistic law of natural language was studied, and Zipf rule was formulated in 1949 (Zipf 1949). The Bayesian theory was well understood and applied on character recognition (Chow 1957). One of the earliest letter-based n-gram was used to correct handwritten FORTRAN codes (Duda and Hart 1968), under the Bayesian theory. Also two famous algorithms were developed. One is the dynamic programming (Bellman 1957) which is widely used in sequential analysis. The other is Rosenblatt's Perceptron (Rosenblatt 1958), the first practical learning machine. Baum and his colleagues laid the foundation of hidden Markov models (HMMs) in the late 1960s (Baum et al. 1970; Baum and Sell 1968; Baum and Eagon 1967; Baum and Petrie 1966). Herefrom, HMMs had served as a robust and efficient tool for signal processing and pattern recognition. In addition, the theory of handwriting generating was carried out by MacDonald in 1964 (MacDonald 1964). The motor theory had inspired the following studies on handwriting synthesizing and recognition.

Chinese character recognition was first addressed in 1966. Casey and Nagy from IBM conducted their celebrated work on printed Chinese character recognition (Casey and Nagy 1966). They proposed a two-stage matching framework based on the structure of Chinese characters. Their framework was widely adopted since then. The pioneer works on online Chinese character recognition were also done in the same year. Two groups independently studied the interesting task and they both employed matching strategy. In one scheme proposed by Liu from MIT (Liu 1966), character recognition is achieved by two types of features regarding Chinese characters: the stroke counting of 19 predefined types, the first and last strokes. In another scheme presented by Zobrak from University of Pittsburgh (Zobrak 1966), feature vectors were derived from trajectory directions, and its weighting vector of each prototype was developed using a Perceptron-like procedure. Inspired by those endeavors, the recognition of printed Japanese Kanji was initialized by Japanese researchers in late 1960s.

1.3.2 Foundation Period (1970s)

In 1977, Thosiba built a printed Kanji recognition system (Wu 2000). It could deal with 2000 Chinese characters. In the late 1970s, researchers in China began to study the printed and online handprinted character recognition (Dai et al. 2007). Different perspectives were taken to identify printed Chinese characters. Stallings provided a structural analysis and encoding scheme (Stallings 1971); Nakano studied the projection feature (Nakano et al. 1973); Yamamoto developed a multiresolution matching scheme (Yamamoto et al. 1973); Transformations, such as Fourier, Rapid, were used to extract features (Wang and Shiau 1973). In the recognition of online Chinese characters, schemes, ranging from analysis-by-synthesis (Yoshida and Eden 1973) to slope and length encoding (Chang and Lo 1973), were reported.

Handful insights derived in this period greatly pushed modern Chinese character recognition forward. A binarization method, Otsu algorithm (Otsu 1979), was published in 1979, which was often used to convert the gray images to black and white ones. The character normalization (Casey 1970) and blurring (Iijima et al. 1972) were first proposed and would become the indispensible steps for the efficient directional feature extraction (Yasuda and Fujisawa 1979), though their power after integration was exposed decades later. The first hand printed Chinese character (Kanji) database, ETL-8 (Mori et al. 1979), was released in the late 1970s. ETL-8 had been used extensively from then on. Moreover, the linguistic postprocessing was verified in the speech recognition field (Jelinek et al. 1975), and would shift to handwriting recognition field because of their resemblance.

Another tendency is about the research scope. First, the less-constrained handwritten numeric was undertaken. In 1976, Suen released a standard database to support such studies (Suen et al. 1980). Second, the handwritten English words (Sayre 1973; Ehrich and Koehler 1975) were tackled after a decade of study on handwritten alphanumeric. In 1979, there also appeared a segmentation free strategy for handwritten words recognition (Farag 1979).

1.3.3 Exploring Period (1980s)

Great leaps were made in the recognition task of printed Chinese characters. In 1985, Fujii manufactured reading product of multifont printed Kanji (Yasuda et al. 1985). Most Japanese Kanji characters have identical shapes to a subset of Chinese characters. In China, the general administration of technology issued a standard set of commonly used Chinese characters, GB2312-1980 (General Administration of Technology of the People's Republic of China 1980). This standard set is further divided into two levels. Level-1 is composed of 3,755 Chinese characters most frequently used in which recognition algorithms are primarily investigated. The amount of commonly used Chinese characters is bigger than Kanji. Borrowing valuable experiences from Japanese researchers, the research on printed Chinese character recognition also made exciting breakthrough (Wu 2000).

As the recognition task of printed Chinese characters has almost been accomplished, the focus then naturally shifted to a more difficult task, recognition of offline handprinted Chinese characters. Since the early 1980s, handprinted Kanji recognition had been pursued by Japanese researchers and intensely impacted the activities in China. In the late 1980s, the offline recognition of handprinted Chinese characters was explored.

For the convenient of the research purpose, an expanded handprinted Kanji database, ETL-9, was released in 1985 (Saito et al. 1985). The amount of Kanji character classes increased from 881 of ETL-8 to 2965 of ETL-9. Similar projects were undertaken in China. In 1988, Institute of Automation of Chinese Academy of Sciences (CASIA) put forward a handprinted Chinese character database named IAAS-4M (Liu et al. 1989; Tu et al. 1991). The character set includes 4,060 symbols and all characters in GB2312-80 level-1 are covered. Almost during the same period, Tsinghua University collected the first subset of THOCR-HCD, which was also handprinted. This resource was continuously updated and there were 13 subsets till now. Unfortunately, it is not available to the public yet.

Feature extraction methods, which were previously used on printed Chinese character recognition, were applied to hand printed Chinese character. For example, peripheral direction contribution (PDC) (Naito et al. 1983), local direction contributivity density (L-DCD) (Hagita et al. 1983), and 2D Hermite polynomial (Maeda et al. 1982) were tried in the early 1980s. To further reduce the variability of handprinted samples, normalization became one of the integrant components of practical handwritten Chinese character recognition.

Considering the difficulties of handprinted Chinese character recognition, use of statistical classification algorithms were widely explored. Before the mid 1980s, methods, such as shifted similarity (Yamada et al. 1981), relaxation matching (Yamamoto 1982), decision trees (Lee et al. 1989; Wang and Suen 1984) and dynamic programming (Yamada 1984), were experimented with limited success. The success of statistical pattern recognition shed light on character recognition field. Neural network (Yao 1988), HMMs, and quadratic function were adapted to deal with Chinese character patterns, yielding the significant models, such as hierarchical neural networks (Mori and Yokosawa 1989), modified quadratic discriminant function (MQDF) (Kimura et al. 1987), regularized discriminant analysis (RDA) (Friedman 1989), and HMMs with maximum mutual information criterion (MMI-HMMs) (Bahl et al. 1986). Statistical algorithms help to hasten the progress of this area.

1.3.4 Transcending Period (1990–2005)

Immense achievements were witnessed in this period. In the early 1990s, Chinese researchers and engineers had deployed recognition products for printed and online handprinted Chinese characters. Hanvon and Wintone were two such companies established for industrial application in 1992. As for offline recognition of handprinted Chinese characters, high accuracies were reported (over 99.4 % on ETL9 and over 98.4 % on IAAS-4M) (Dai et al. 2007). It was thus believed that the problem underlying offline recognition of handwritten Chinese characters was already solved. However, this is not true in hindsight.

We mainly focus on the key progress in the field of handprinted Chinese character recognition. First, dozens of handwritten character databases were collected. In the first year, a Chinese handwritten character database entitled ITRI (Tu et al. 1991; Tang and Suen 1993) was done which was hand-printed by 3,000 people in Taiwan. In 1992, CENPARMI (Suen et al. 1992) and PE92 (Kim et al. 1993, 1996) were reported. The former consists of unconstrained handwritten postcodes sampled from real mail pieces. The latter is a Korean character database written by 1,000 writers [an alternative Korean database is KU-1 (Park et al. 2000)]. Two years later, CEDAR (Hull 1994) and CAMBRIDGE (Senior and Robinson 1998) were released. Similar to CENPARMI, CEDAR is also collected from real mail pieces. What's more, it includes a subset of handwritten city words extracting from mail addresses. CAMBRIDGE is the first handwritten English text database with a large vocabulary, which is written by a single writer in an unconstrained domain and used for writer-dependent handwriting recognition. Following that, one online Kanji character database named TUAT (Nakagawa et al. 1997; Matsumoto et al. 2001) was published in 1997. In 1998, the first version of IAM was put forward (Marti and Bunke 1999), then the second version in 2002 (Marti and Bunke 2002), adapting some ideas from CAMBRIDGE. It is written by multiple writers and the texts for handcopying are progressively taken from the Lancaster-Oslo/Bergen (LOB) corpus. In 1999, a French handwritten database, IRONOFF (Viard-Gaudin et al. 1999), was released. While the characters are recorded in an online manner, they can be transformed into offline versions. In 2000, a handprinted Chinese character database named HCL2000 (Zhang and Guo 2000) and a handwritten Greek database named GRUHD (Kavallieratou et al. 2001) were published. Writers in HCL2000 are asked to write a comprehensive set of the First Level Chinese characters of GB2312-80 and the characters should be carefully written within a preprinted character box. GRUHD consists of two subsets. One includes hand-printed Greek characters and digits, the other an unconstrained Greek poem that can be used to conduct text line segmentation experiments. More recently, a Chinese character database named HK2002 (Ge and Huo 2002; Ge et al. 2002) and an Indian database named ISI (Bhattacharya and Chaudhuri 2005), are reported.

Besides the fundamental databases, all the other components of a Chinese character recognition system were thoroughly investigated. For preprocessing, both 1D and pseudo-2D nonlinear shape normalization methods (Liu and Marukawa 2005, 2004; Liu et al. 2003b) were designed to relieve the variability of writing. Similarly, the equalization of variability can be achieved by elastic cells (Jin and Wei 1999), zoning the samples adaptively. As for feature extraction, robustness of directional features (Kawamura et al. 1992; Chen et al. 1997), such as gradient features (Srikantan et al. 1996), were assured in both online and offline Chinese character recognition (Liu et al. 2003a). To reduce the computation cost, endeavors were taken to merge shape normalization and feature extraction into a single step (Hamanaka et al. 1993; Liu 2007). After the feature vector was extracted, the variable transformation might make the vector more Gaussian-like, facilitating the nearest neighbor and Gaussian classifiers (Fukunaga 1990;

Wakabayashi et al. 1993). For classifier design, a wide range of statistical methods were investigated. They broadly fall into three different types: (1) generative models, such as HMMs (Jeng et al. 1990; Feng et al. 2002) and MQDF; (2) discriminative models, including neural network (LeCun et al. 1998), learning vector quantization (LVQ) (Kohonen 1990; Sato and Yamada 1995); (3) discriminatively trained generative models, such as HMMs with minimum classification error (MCE) criterion (MCE-HMMs) (Juang et al. 1992; Ge et al. 2002), MMI-HMMs (Nopsuwanchai 2005) and MCE-MQDF (Liu et al. 2004). Ensemble of multiple classifiers was further used to improve the recognition accuracy, both in small-category tasks (Xu et al. 1992; Bertolami and Bunke 2005; Mohamed and Gader 1996; Gunter and Bunke 2005) and large-category tasks (Hao et al. 1997; Lin et al. 1998). For the postprocessing step, the linguistic constraints especially n-gram were utilized to resolve ambiguity and correct errors (Li et al. 2002, 2004, 2005; Li and Tan 2004a, b; Wong and Chan 1999; Rosenfeld 2000).

Third, the recognition scope was shifted to handwritten sentence (or text line) in English handwriting recognition (Marti and Bunke 2000). Segmentation-free strategies based on HMMs were used to deal with such task (Vinciarelli et al. 2004). For informative surveys on this topic, please refer to Bunke (2003), Bortolozzi et al. (2005) and Ploetz and Fink (2009). In Chinese character recognition field, studies on handwritten sentence were merely conducted on constrained domains, for example, handwritten check reading (Gao et al. 1999) and address interpretation (Xue et al. 2001). Their efforts were taken mainly on character segmentation (Xue et al. 2001; Liu et al. 2002; Zhao et al. 2003; Li and Shi 2004; Liang and Shi 2005; Jiang et al. 2006).

1.3.5 Regenerative Period (Since 2006)

The handwritten Chinese character recognition problem is still unsolved, though very high accuracies have been reported on databases of constrained writing styles. In the recent handwriting recognition competition, the accuracy on unconstrained handwritten character samples is less than 93 % (Liu et al. 2010). On the other hand, real-life Chinese handwritten documents may present complex text lines, instead of easily separated characters. To meet the overwhelming challenge, we should strive hard to make greater progress.

The recognition scope has been shifted to the unconstrained Chinese handwriting recognition. With the first unconstrained handwriting database, HIT-MW database (Su et al. 2007a, 2006), Chinese researchers started to overcome the problems inherent in the practical reading machine for Chinese handwriting. It includes 853 legible Chinese handwriting samples from more than 780 participants with a systematic philosophy. Inspired by HIT-MW database, another three Chinese handwriting databases are built recently: SCUT-COUCH (Jin et al. 2011), HIT-OR3C (Zhou et al. 2010), and CASIA-OLHDB/CASIA-HWDB (Liu et al. 2011a). Among them, HIT-MW database and CASIA-HWDB can facilitate the offline tasks while others can support the online tasks. Provided with these training samples, sophisticated learning algorithms can be investigated.

Available recognition methods can be dichotomized: segmentation-free strategy and integrated segmentation-recognition strategy. Both of them have yielded inspiring results. The former has been pursued with HMMs to read Chinese handwriting since 2007 (Su et al. 2007b). HMM-based handwriting recognition has the merit that the model parameters can be trained with string samples without annotation of character boundaries. Within this strategy, activities have taken place in feature extraction methods (Su et al. 2008), the string sample synthesizing (Su and Liu 2010), linguistic correction and ensemble of distinct approaches (Su et al. 2009; Su 2008). Besides HMMs, there are English handwriting recognition systems based on recurrent neural networks (Graves et al. 2009; Graves 2012). Hopefully, such systems can be transferred to Chinese handwriting recognition. To the latter, it is initially proposed to tackle handwritten numeric strings (Fujisawa et al. 1992). Recently, it is transferred to Chinese handwriting recognition (Wang et al. 2012b; Li and Jin 2011). The strategy can incorporate multiple contexts, for example, language models (Zou et al. 2008; Wang et al. 2009, 2012a), geometric models (Yin et al. 2010; Zhou et al. 2007), and confidence measurements from character-level classifier (Wang et al. 2012b). Currently, character over-segmentation (Xu et al. 2011; Li et al. 2008) becomes one of the bottlenecks and efforts to remove this are underway.

A reliable way to improve the robustness is discriminative learning. The character models can be discriminatively trained either in character-level or string-level manner. Character-level training infers parameters from isolated character samples. On the one hand, the generative models, such as MQDF, are retrained using discriminative learning criteria. Group led by Huo proposes a sample-separation margin to rectify regular minimum classification error criterion (He and Huo 2008; Wang and Huo 2010); Su and Liu present an efficient dynamic margin-based algorithm within Perceptron learning framework (Su et al. 2011); Wang and Ding iteratively train character models based on the sample weighting, considering the relationship between the sample and decision boundary (Wang et al. 2011a, b). On the other hand, discriminative models, such as convolutional neural network (CNN) (Ciresan et al. 2011), may be appliable to large-category learning tasks, if parallel computing facilities are used [as revealed in (Liu et al. 2011b)]. Unlikely, string-level training concatenates sub-unit models together to form a string and the underlying parameters are estimated in an embedding way. To compensate the great variability in unconstrained Chinese handwriting, the character models can be adjusted on Chinese string samples aiming at optimizing the MCE criterion (Chen et al. 2010). In addition, conditional random field (CRF) is pursued on online Chinese handwriting recognition with pleasing result (Zhou et al. 2009), which is a discriminative model in nature.

In the relevant field, such as speech recognition and English handwriting recognition, some researchers developed margin-based methods for HMMs. Sha has derived a convex objective function with large margin constraint through relaxation (Sha 2007; Sha and Saul 2007a, b). In the following works, they solved the parameter optimization of HMMs using Perceptron with margin for scalability (Cheng et al. 2010; Cheng 2011). Recently, they worked out a rigid guarantee, decaying the size of margin (Keshet et al. 2011). Parallel attempt is also undertaken to express the large margin HMMs as nonconvex but precise objective function (Do and Artières 2009). Armed with regularized bundle solvers, their advantages are demonstrated both on speech and handwriting recognition (Do 2010). Whether above methods were applicable to Chinese handwriting is still not clear.

There are some other techniques that have been utilized to improve performance in literature. Synthesizing more training samples is widely used in both character recognition (Leung and Leung 2009) and handwriting recognition (Bunke 2003). Recently, such investigations are conducted both on offline (Chen et al. 2010; Su and Liu 2010) and online (Chen et al. 2011) Chinese handwriting recognition. For a scalable training, active set tricks (Su et al. 2011) and distributed (including parallel computation) training (Ciresan et al. 2011; McDonald et al. 2010) deserve exploratory experiments. For the sake of a practical large-category recognizer, researchers also keep attention on the model compression (Long and Jin 2008; Wang and Huo 2011).

1.4 Evaluation Metrics

Standard handwriting databases should be used to evaluate newly developed algorithms. Usually, the character segmentation and recognition rates are measured.

1.4.1 Character Segmentation Rates

To a character segment, its segmentation decision falls into "right" or "wrong" exclusively. Compared to the concepts of relevance and irrelevance in information retrieval (Mikolajczyk and Schmid 2005), we can define segmentation correct rate (SCR) and segmentation precision rate (SPR). The SCR provides the fraction of correct characters that are segmented by the character segmentation algorithm:

$$\text{SCR} = \frac{N_s}{N_t} \times 100\,\%, \tag{1.1}$$

where N_S is the number of correctly segmented characters and N_t is the total number of characters in the reference text. In another way, the SPR describe the percentage of character segments that are correctly extracted:

$$\text{SPR} = \frac{N_s}{N_b} \times 100\,\%, \tag{1.2}$$

where N_b is the total number of character segments given by the segmentation algorithm.

In addition, we define segmentation bias rate (SBR) to reveal its tendency in over-segmentation and under-segmentation:

$$\text{SBR} = \frac{N_b - N_t}{N_t} \times 100\,\%. \tag{1.3}$$

Merely, using any one or two of above measures may be not enough to show the ability of the character segmentation algorithm. Instead, they should be evaluated and considered together.

1.4.2 Recognition Rates

The output of certain recognizer is compared with the reference transcription and two metrics, the recognition correct rate (CR) and recognition accurate rate (AR), are calculated to evaluate the results. Supposing the number of substitution errors (S_e), deletion errors (D_e), and insertion errors (I_e) are known, CR and AR are defined respectively as:

$$\begin{cases} \text{CR} = \dfrac{N_t - D_e - S_e}{N_t} \times 100\,\% \\[3mm] \text{AR} = \dfrac{N_t - D_e - S_e - I_e}{N_t} \times 100\,\% \end{cases}. \tag{1.4}$$

In general, CR is nonnegative while AR may be negative if there are over many insertion errors.

1.5 Organization

This book intends to provide an algorithmic perspective on Chinese handwriting recognition. The contents covered are illustrated in Fig. 1.3. According to the authors, it is necessary to understand simple methods before trying to grasp more complex ones. In view of layers, the techniques are categorized into basic and sophisticated approaches. The basic techniques are enclosed with a solid circle and they comprise the fundamental Chinese handwriting recognizer. Sophisticated ones are put between the solid circle and the solid rectangle, improving the fundamental recognizers. As a base, evaluation metrics, handwriting database and text corpus are supporting essentials. On the other hand, the contents can also be subdivided by two diagonals into four disjoined parts. They are the indispensible building blocks of a practical reading machine for Chinese handwriting.

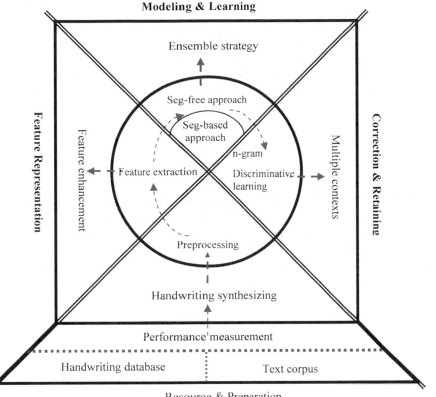

Fig. 1.3 Research contents of this book

The remainder of the book is organized as follows. In Chap. 2, we will provide a dedicated scheme for collecting the HIT-MW database. The database is collected from more than 780 participants in an unconstrained manner. The writers are mainly college students and the department distribution and gender distribution of them are near to those of real distributions of college students. The underlying texts of the HIT-MW database are randomly sampled from People's Daily corpus in a systematic way. As a result, a high character coverage on People's Daily corpus (with approximately 80 million characters) is obtained (the coverage rate is 99.33 %). The HIT-MW database can be seen as a representative subset of real Chinese handwriting.

The next chapters aim to develop reading machines for Chinese handwriting from both segmentation-free strategy and integrated segmentation-recognition strategy. The integrated segmentation-recognition strategy is studied in Chap. 3. The input image is first over-segmented into primitive segments, and then the consecutive segments are combined into candidate patterns. The embedded classifier is used to classify all the candidate patterns in segmentation lattice.

According to path evaluation function, the system outputs the optimal path in segmentation-recognition lattice, which is the final recognition result. The basic structure of the system is studied first under Bayesian framework. For better generalization performance, dynamic margin regularization is proposed within Perceptron learning. To relieve the heavy burden in training process, we train the MQDF classifer using active set technique. Moreover, string-level training is also utilized to adjust the initial MQDF on synthetic string samples. The learning process is accomplished by stochastic gradient descent aiming at optimizing the MCE criterion. In addition, a bigram language model is incorporated for a reliable improvement.

Finally, Chaps. 4 and 5 investigate the continuous density HMM-based recognition system (CDHMM) where each character is modeled by a CDHMM. The parameters of character HMMs are estimated by embedded Baum-Welch algorithm on text line samples. During decoding the optimal string, above character HMMs are utilized to facilitate the search process. The HMM-based segmentation-free strategy for Chinese handwriting recognition has the advantage of training without annotation of character boundaries. The enhancement of feature representation, synthesizing more string samples, incorporating linguistic constraints, ensemble of distinct recognizers and utilizing minimum phone error (MPE) criterion are used to improve the robustness of the system. The basis of the system is presented in Chap. 4, while the further enhancements are given in Chap. 5.

References

L. Bahl, P. Brown, P. Souza, R. Mercer, Maximum mutual information estimation of hidden Markov model parameters for speech recognition, in *IEEE International Conference on Acoustics, Speech and Signal Processing* (1986)

L.E. Baum, J.A. Eagon, An inequality with applications to statistical estimation for probabilistic functions of Markov processes and to a model for ecology. Bull. Am. Math. Soc. **73**, 360–363 (1967)

L.E. Baum, T. Petrie, Statistical inference for probabilistic functions of finite state Markov chains. Ann. Math. Stat. **37**(6), 1554–1563 (1966)

L.E. Baum, T. Petrie, G. Soules, N. Weiss, A maximization technique occurring in the statistical analysis of probabilistic functions of Markov chains. Ann. Math. Stat. **41**, 164–171 (1970)

L.E. Baum, G.R. Sell, Growth transformations for functions on manifolds. Pac. J. Math. **27**(2), 211–227 (1968)

R. Bellman, *Dynamic Programming* (Princeton University Press, New Jersey, 1957)

R. Bertolami, H, Bunke, Ensemble methods for handwritten text line recognition systems, in *IEEE International Conference on Systems, Man and Cybernetics*, ed. by H. Bunke, pp. 2334–2339 (2005)

U. Bhattacharya, B.B. Chaudhuri, Databases for research on recognition of handwritten characters of Indian scripts, in *Proceedings of the 8th International Conference on Document Analysis and Recognition*, Seoul, pp. 789–793 (2005)

F. Bortolozzi, Jr S. Aires, L.S. Oliveira, M. Morita, *Recent Advances in Handwriting Recognition*, ed. by U. Pal, S.K. Parui, B.B. Chaudhuri. Document Analysis (Allied Publishers Pvt. Ltd, Kolkata, 2005), pp. 1–30

H. Bunke, Recognition of cursive roman handwriting—past, present and future, in *ICDAR* (2003)

R. Casey, G. Nagy, Recognition of printed Chinese characters. IEEE Trans. Electron. Comput. **EC-15**(1), 91–101 (1966)

R.G. Casey, Moment normalization of handprinted characters. IBM J. Res. Dev. **14**(5), 548–557 (1970). doi:10.1147/rd.145.0548

S. Chang, D. Lo, An experimental system for the recognition of handwritten Chinese characters, in *Proceedings of the 1st International Symposium on Computers and Chinese Input/Output Systems*, pp. 257–267 (1973)

B. Chen, B. Zhu, M. Nakagawa, Effects of generating a large amount of artificial patterns for online handwritten Japanese character recognition, in *ICDAR* pp. 663–667 (2011)

X. Chen, T.-H. Su, T.-W. Zhang, Discriminative training of MQDF classifier on synthetic Chinese string samples, in *Chinese Conference on Patten Recognition (CCPR)* (2010)

Y. Chen, X. Ding, Y. Wu, Off-line handwritten Chinese character recognition based on crossing line feature, in *Proceedings of the 4th International Conference on Document Analysis and Recognition*, Ulm, pp. 206–210 (1997)

C.-C. Cheng, Online Learning of Large Margin Hidden Markov Models for Automatic Speech Recognition. Ph.D. thesis, University of California, San Diego, 2011

C.C. Cheng, F. Sha, L.K. Saul, Online learning and acoustic feature adaptation in large-margin hidden Markov models. IEEE J. Sel. Top. Sign. Process. **4**(6), 926–942 (2010)

C.K. Chow, An optimum character recognition system using decision functions. IRE Trans. Electron. Comput. **EC-6**(4), 247–254 (1957)

D.C. Ciresan, U. Meier, J. Masci, L.M. Gambardella, J. Schmidhuber, Flexible, high performance convolutional neural networks for image classification, in *Proceedings of the 22nd International Joint Conference on Artificial Intelligence* (2011)

R. Dai, C. Liu, B. Xiao, Chinese character recognition: history, status and prospects. Front. Comput. Sci. China **1**(2), 126–136 (2007)

T.-M.-T. Do, Regularized bundle methods for large-scale learning problems with an application to large margin training of hidden Markov models. Ph.D. thesis, LIP6, Paris, 2010

T.-M.-T. Do, T. Artières, Large margin training for hidden Markov models with partially observed states, in *International Conference on Machine Learning* (2009)

R.O. Duda, P.E. Hart, Experiments in the recognition of hand-printed text, part II-context analysis, in *Proceedings of the Fall Joint Computer Conference*, pp. 1139–1139 (1968)

R. Ehrich, K. Koehler, Experiments in the contextual recognition of cursive script. IEEE Trans. Comput. **C-24**(2), 182–194 (1975)

R. Farag, Word-level recognition of cursive script. IEEE Trans. Comput. **C-28**(2), 172–175 (1979)

B. Feng, X. Ding, Y. Wu, Chinese handwriting recognition using Hidden Markov Models, in *Proceedings of the 16th International Conference on Pattern Recognition*, Quebec, pp. 212–215 (2002)

J.H. Friedman, Regularized discriminant analysis. J. Am. Stat. Assoc. **84**(405), 165–175 (1989)

H. Fujisawa, Y. Nakano, K. Kurino, Segmentation methods for character recognition: from segmentation to document structure analysis. Proc. IEEE **80**(7), 1079–1092 (1992). doi:10.1109/5.156471

K. Fukunaga, *Introduction to Statistical Pattern Recognition*, 2nd edn. (Academic Press, San Diego, 1990)

J. Gao, X. Ding, Y. Wu, A segmentation algorithm for handwritten Chinese character strings, in *Proceedings of the 5th International Conference on Document Analysis and Recognition*, pp. 633–636 (1999)

Y. Ge, Q. Huo, A comparative study of several modeling approaches for large vocabulary offline recognition of handwritten Chinese characters, in *International Conference on Pattern Recognition*, pp. 85–88 (IEEE Computer Society, Quebec, 2002)

Y. Ge, Q. Huo, Z.D. Feng, Offline recognition of handwritten Chinese characters using Gabor features, CDHMM modeling and MCE training, in *Proceedings of the IEEE International Conference on Acoustics, Speech and Signal Processing*, Orlando, pp. 1053–1056 (2002)

General Administration of Technology of the People's Republic of China, *Code of Chinese Graphic Character Set for Information Interchange–Primary Set* (Standard Press of China, Beijing, 1980). (in Chinese)

A. Graves, *Supervised Sequence Labelling with Recurrent Neural Networks* (Springer, Heidelberg, 2012)

A. Graves, M. Liwicki, S. Fernández, R. Bertolami, H. Bunke, J. Schmidhuber, A novel connectionist system for unconstrained handwriting recognition. IEEE Trans. Pattern Anal. Mach. Intell. **31**(5), 855–868 (2009)

E.C. Greanias, *Some important factors in the practical utilization of optical character readers* ed. by G.L. Fischer. Optical Character Recognition (McGregor and Wemer, Washington, 1962), pp. 129–146

S. Gunter, H. Bunke, Off-line cursive handwriting recognition using multiple classifier systems— on the influence of vocabulary, ensemble, and training set size. Opt. Lasers Eng. **43**(3–5), 437–454 (2005)

N. Hagita, S. Naito, I. Masuda, Handprinted Kanji characters recognition based on pattern matching method, in *Proceedings of the International Conference on Text Processing with a Large Character Set*, pp. 169–114 (1983)

M. Hamanaka, K. Yamada, J. Tsukumo, Normalization-cooperated feature extraction method for handprinted Kanji character recognition, in *Proceedings of the 3rd International Workshop on Frontiers of Handwriting Recognition*, pp. 343–348 (1993)

H. Hao, X. Xiao, R. Dai, Handwritten Chinese character recognition by metasynthetic approach. Pattern Recogn. **30**(8), 1321–1328 (1997)

T. He, Q. Huo, A study of a new misclassification measure for minimum classification error training of prototype-based pattern classifiers, in *IEEE International Conference on Pattern Recognition*, pp. 1–4 (2008)

W. Highleyman, An analog method for character recognition. IRE Trans. Electron. Comput. **EC-10**, 502–512 (1961)

J. Hull, A database for handwritten text recognition research. IEEE Trans. Pattern Anal. Mach. Intell. **16**(5), 550–554 (1994)

I. Iijima, Y. Okumura, K. Kuwabara, New process of character recognition using sieving method. Inf. Control Res. **1**(1), 30–35 (1963)

T. Iijima, H. Genchi, K. Mori, A theoretical study of pattern identification by matching method, in *Proceedings of the 1st USA-JAPAN Computer Conference*, Tokyo, pp. 42–48 (1972)

F. Jelinek, L.R. Bahl, R.L. Mercer, Design of a linguistic statistical decoder for recognition of continuous speech. IEEE Trans. Inf. Theory **IT-21**(3), 250–256 (1975)

B.-S. Jeng, M.-W. Chang, S.-W. Sun, C.-H. Shih, T.-M. Wu, Optical Chinese character recognition with a hidden Markov model classifier—a novel approach. Electron. Lett. **26**(18), 1530–1531 (1990)

Y. Jiang, X. Ding, Z. Ren, Substring alignment method for lexicon based handwritten Chinese string recognition and its application to address line recognition, in *Proceedings of the 18th International Conference on Pattern Recognition*, pp. 683–686 (2006)

L. Jin, Y. Gao, G. Liu, Y. Li, K. Ding, SCUT-COUCH2009–a comprehensive online unconstrained Chinese handwriting database and benchmark evaluation. Int. J. Doc. Anal. Recogn. **14**(1), 53–64 (2011)

L. Jin, G. Wei, Handwritten Chinese character recognition with directional decomposition cellular features. J. Circuit Syst. Comput. **8**(4), 517–524 (1999)

B.H. Juang, W. Hou, C.H. Lee, Minimum classification error rate methods for speech recognition. IEEE Trans. Speech Audio Process. **5**(3), 257–265 (1992)

E. Kavallieratou, N. Liolios, E. Koutsogeorgos, N. Fakotakis, G. Kokkinakis, The GRUHD database of Greek unconstrained handwriting, in *Proceedings of the 6th International Conference on Document Analysis and Recognition*, Seattle, pp. 561–565 (2001)

A. Kawamura, K. Yura, T. Hayama, On-line recognition of freely handwritten Japanese characters using directional feature densities, in *Proceedings of 11th ICPR*, pp. 183–186 (1992)

J. Keshet, C.-C. Cheng, M. Stoehr, D. McAllester, L.K. Saul, Direct error rate minimization of hidden Markov models, in *IEEE International Conference on Acoustics, Speech and Signal Processing* (2011)

D.H. Kim, Y.S. Hwang, S.T. Park, E.J. Kim, S.H. Paek, S.Y. Bang, Handwritten Korean character image database PE92, in *Proceedings of the 2nd International Conference on Document Analysis and Recognition*, Tsukuba, pp. 470–473 (1993)

D.H. Kim, Y.S. Hwang, S.T. Park, E.J. Kim, S.H. Paek, S.Y. Bang, Handwritten Korean character image database PE92. IEICE Trans. Inf. Syst. **E79-D**(7), 943–950 (1996)

F. Kimura, K. Takashina, S. Tsuruoka, Y. Miyake, Modified quadratic discriminant functions and the application to Chinese character recognition. IEEE Trans. Pattern Anal. Mach. Intell. **9**(1), 149–153 (1987)

T. Kohonen, The self-organizing map. Proc. IEEE **78**(9), 1464–1480 (1990)

Y. LeCun, L. Bottou, Y. Bengio, P. Haffner, Gradient-based learning applied to document recognition. Proc. IEEE **86**(1), 2278–2324 (1998)

S. Lee, Z. Chang, W. Wu, A. Huang, B. Ye, Radical extraction methods for processing and recognition of Chinese characters, in *International Symposium on Computer. Architecture and Digital Signal Processing*, pp. 480–483 (1989)

K.-C. Leung, C.-H. Leung, Recognition of handwritten Chinese characters by combining regularization, fisher's discriminant and distorted sample generation, in *10th ICDAR*, pp. 1026–1030 (2009)

G.-H. Li, P.-F. Shi, An approach to offline handwritten Chinese character recognition based on segment evaluation of adaptive duration. J. Zhejiang Univ. Sci. **5**(11), 1392–1397 (2004)

N.-X. Li, L.-W. Jin, A Bayesian-based method of unconstrained handwritten offline Chinese text line recognition. Int. J. Doc. Anal. Recogn. (IJDAR) (2012). doi:10.1007/s10032-011-0178-0

N. Li, Writer-independent unconstrained handwritten offline Chinese text line recognition. Ph.D. thesis, South China University of Technology, Guangzhou 2010 (in Chinese)

N. Li, X. Gao, L. Jin, Curved segmentation path generation for unconstrained handwritten Chinese text lines, in *IEEE Asia Pacific Conference on Circuits and Systems*, pp. 501–505 (2008)

Y. Li, X. Ding, C.L. Tan, Combining character-based bigrams with word-based bigrams in contextual postprocessing for Chinese script recognition. ACM Trans. Asian Lang. Inf. Process. **1**(4), 297–309 (2002)

Y. Li, C.L. Tan, An empirical study of statistical language models for contextual post-processing of Chinese script recognition, in *Proceedings of the 9th International Workshop on Frontiers in Handwriting Recognition*, pp. 257–262 (2004a)

Y. Li, C.L. Tan, Influence of language models and candidate set size on contextual post-processing for Chinese script recognition, in *Proceedings of the 17th International Conference on Pattern Recognition*, pp. 537–540 (2004b)

Y. Li, C.L. Tan, X. Ding, A hybrid post-processing system for offline handwritten Chinese script recognition. Pattern Anal. Appl. **8**(3), 272–286 (2005)

Y. Li, C.L. Tan, X. Ding, C. Liu, Contextual post-processing based on the confusion matrix in offline handwritten Chinese script recognition. Pattern Recogn. **37**(9), 1901–1912 (2004)

Z. Liang, P. Shi, A metasynthetic approach for segmenting handwritten Chinese character strings. Pattern Recogn. Lett. **26**(10), 1498–1511 (2005)

X. Lin, X. Ding, M. Chen, R. Zhang, Y. Wu, Adaptive confidence transform based classifier combination for Chinese character recognition. Pattern Recogn. Lett. **19**(10), 975–988 (1998)

C.-L. Liu, Normalization-cooperated gradient feature extraction for handwritten character recognition. IEEE Trans. Pattern Anal. Mach. Intell. **29**(8), 1465–1469 (2007)

C.-L. Liu, *Handwritten Chinese Character Recognition: Effects of Shape Normalization and Feature Extraction*, ed. by S. Jaeger, D. Doermann. Arabic and Chinese Handwriting Recognition, LNCS (Springer, Berlin, 2008), pp. 104–128

C.-L. Liu, M. Koga, H. Fujisawa, Lexicon-driven segmentation and recognition of handwritten character strings for Japanese address reading. IEEE Trans. Pattern Anal. Mach. Intell. **24**(11), 1425–1437 (2002)

C.-L. Liu, K. Marukawa, Global shape normalization for handwritten Chinese character recognition: a new method, in *Proceedings of the 9th International Workshop on Frontiers in Handwriting Recognition*, pp. 300–305 (2004)

C.-L. Liu, K. Marukawa, Pseudo two-dimensional shape normalization methods for handwritten Chinese character recognition. Pattern Recogn. **38**(12), 2242–2255 (2005)

C.-L. Liu, K. Nakashima, H. Sako, H. Fujisawa, Handwritten digit recognition: benchmarking of state-of-the-art techniques. Pattern Recogn. **36**(10), 2271–2285 (2003a). doi:10.1016/s0031-3203(03)00085-2

C.-L. Liu, H. Sako, H. Fujisawa, Handwritten Chinese character recognition: alternatives to nonlinear normalization, in *Proceedings of the 7th International Conference on Document Analysis and Recognition,* Edinburgh, Scotland, pp. 524–528 (2003b)

C.-L. Liu, H. Sako, H. Fujisawa, Discriminative learning quadratic discriminant function for handwriting recognition. IEEE Trans. Neural Netw. **15**(2), 430–444 (2004)

C.-L. Liu, F. Yin, D.-H. Wang, Q.-F. Wang, Chinese handwriting recognition contest 2010, in *Chinese Conference on Patten Recognition (CCPR)* (2010)

C.-L. Liu, F. Yin, D.-H. Wang, Q.-F. Wang, CASIA online and offline Chinese handwriting databases. in ICDAR 37–41 (2011a)

C.-L. Liu, F. Yin, Q.-F. Wang, D.-H. Wang, Chinese handwriting recognition competition, in *International Conference on Document Analysis and Recognition* (2011b)

J.-H. Liu, Real time Chinese handwriting recognition. EE thesis, Massachusetts Institute of Technology, Cambridge, 1966

Y.J. Liu, J.W. Tai, J. Liu, An introduction to the 4 million handwriting Chinese character samples library, in *Proceedings of the International Conference on Chinese Computing and Orient Language Processing*, Changsha, pp. 94–97 (1989)

T. Long, L. Jin, Building compact MQDF classifier for large character set recognition by subspace distribution sharing. Pattern Recogn. **41**(9), 2916–2925 (2008)

J.S. MacDonald, Experimental studies of handwriting signals. Ph.D. thesis, Massachusetts Institute of Technology, Cambridge, 1964

K. Maeda, Y. Kurosawa, H. Asada, K. Sakai, S. Watanabe, Handprinted Kanji recognition by pattern matching method, in *International Conference on Pattern Recognition*, pp. 789–792 (1982)

U.V. Marti, H. Bunke, A full English sentence database for off-line handwriting recognition, in *Proceedings of the 5th International Conference on Document Analysis and Recognition*, Bangalore, pp. 705–708 (1999)

U.V. Marti, H. Bunke, Handwritten sentence recognition, in *Proceedings of the 15th International Conference on Pattern Recognition*, pp. 463–466 (2000)

U.V. Marti, H. Bunke, The IAM-database: an English sentence database for off-line handwriting recognition. Int. J. Doc. Anal. Recogn. **5**(1), 39–46 (2002)

K. Matsumoto, T. Fukushima, M. Nakagawa, Collection and analysis of on-line handwritten Japanese character patterns, in *Proceedings of the 6th ICDAR*, pp. 496–500 (2001)

R. McDonald, K. Hall, G. Mann, Distributed training strategies for the structured perceptron, in *North American Association for Computational Linguistics (NAACL)*, pp. 456–464 (2010)

K. Mikolajczyk, C. Schmid, A performance evaluation of local descriptors. IEEE Trans. Pattern Anal. Mach. Intell. **27**(10), 1615–1630 (2005)

M. Mohamed, P. Gader, Handwritten word recognition using segmentation-free hidden Markov modeling and segmentation-based dynamic programming techniques. IEEE Trans. Pattern Anal. Mach. Intell. **18**(5), 548–554 (1996)

S. Mori, K. Yamamoto, H. Yamada, T. Saito, On a handprinted Kyoiku-Kanji character data base. Bull. Electrotech. Lab. **43**(11–12), 752–773 (1979)

Y. Mori, K. Yokosawa, Neural networks that learn to discriminate similar Kanji characters. in Adv. Neural Inf. Process. Syst. **1**, 332–339 (1989)

J.H. Munson, Experiments in the recognition of hand-printed text, part l-character recognition, in *Proceedings of the Fall Joint Computer Conference*, San Francisco, pp. 1125–1125 (1968)

S. Naito, N. Hagita, I. Masuda, Handprinted Kanji recognition by feature matching methods and its application to personal OCR, in *IEEE Conference on Computer Vision and Pattern Recognition*, pp. 297–302 (1983)

M. Nakagawa, T. Higashiyama, Y. Yamanaka, S. Sawada, L. Higashigawa, K. Akiyama, On-line handwritten character pattern database sampled in a sequence of sentences without any writing instructions, in *Proceedings of the Fourth International Conference on Document Analysis and Recognition*, Ulm, pp. 376–381 (1997)

Y. Nakano, K. Nakata, Y. Uchikura, A. Nakajima, Improvement of Chinese character recognition using projection profiles, in *International Conference on Pattern Recognition*, pp. 172–178 (1973)

R. Nopsuwanchai, Discriminative training methods and their applications to handwriting recognition. Ph.D. thesis, University of Cambridge, Cambridge, 2005

N. Otsu, A threshold selection method from gray-level histogram. IEEE Trans. Syst. Man Cybern. **SMC-9**(1), 62–66 (1979)

J.S. Park, H.J. Kang, S.W. Lee, Automatic quality measurement of gray-scale handwriting based on extended average entropy, in *Proceedings of the 15th International Conference on Pattern Recognition*, Barcelona, pp. 426–429 (2000)

T. Ploetz, G.A. Fink, Markov models for offline handwriting recognition: a survey. Int. J. Doc. Anal. Recogn. **12**(4), 269–298 (2009)

W.S. Rohland, Character sensing system. USA Patent 2877951, Mar 1959 (1956)

F. Rosenblatt, The perceptron: a probabilistic model for information storage and organization in the brain. Psychol. Rev. **65**(6), 386–408 (1958). doi:10.1037/h0042519

R. Rosenfeld, Two decades of statistical language modeling: where do we go from here? Proc. IEEE **88**(8), 1270–1278 (2000)

T. Saito, H. Yamada, K. Yamamoto, On the data base ETL9 of handprinted characters in JIS Chinese characters and its analysis. IEICE Trans. **J68-D**(4), 757–764 (1985)

A. Sato, K. Yamada, Generalized learning vector quantization. in Adv. Neural Inf. Process. Syst. **7**, 423–429 (1995)

K. Sayre, Machine recognition of handwritten words: a project report. Pattern Recogn. **5**(3), 213–228 (1973)

A.W. Senior, A.J. Robinson, An off-line cursive handwriting recognition system. IEEE Trans. Pattern Anal. Mach. Intell. **20**(3), 309–321 (1998)

F. Sha, Large margin training of acoustic models for speech recognition. Ph.D. thesis, University of Pennsylvania, Pennsylvania, 2007

F. Sha, L.K. Saul, Comparison of large margin training to other discriminative methods for phonetic recognition by hidden Markov models, in *IEEE International Conference on Acoustics, Speech and Signal Processing*, Honolulu, HI, pp. 313–316 (2007a)

F. Sha, L.K. Saul, Large margin hidden Markov models for automatic speech recognition. Adv. Neural Inf. Process. Syst. **19**, 1249–1256 (2007b)

G. Srikantan, S.W. Lam, S.N. Srihari, Gradient-based contour encoding for character recognition. Pattern Recogn. **29**(7), 1147–1160 (1996). doi:10.1016/0031-3203(95)00146-8

W. Stallings, Computer analysis of printed Chinese characters. Ph.D. thesis, Massachusetts Institute of Technology, Cambridge, 1971

T.-H. Su, Off-line recognition of Chinese handwriting: from isolated character to realistic text. Ph.D. theses, Harbin Institute of Technology, Harbin, 2008 (in Chinese)

T.-H. Su, C.-L. Liu, Improving HMM-based Chinese handwriting recognition using delta features and synthesized string samples, in *International Conference on Frontiers in Handwriting Recognition* (2010)

T.-H. Su, C.-L. Liu, X.-Y. Zhang, Perceptron learning of modified quadratic discriminant function. in ICDAR (2011)

T.-H. Su, T.-W. Zhang, D.-J. Guan, HIT-MW dataset for offline Chinese handwritten text recognition, in *Proceedings of the 10th International Workshop on Frontiers in Handwriting Recognition*, La Baule, INRIA–CCSd–CNRS, pp. 574–578 (2006)

T.-H. Su, T.-W. Zhang, D.-J. Guan, Corpus-based HIT-MW database for offline recognition of general-purpose Chinese handwritten text. Int. J. Doc. Anal. Recogn. **10**(1), 27–38 (2007a)

T.-H. Su, T.-W. Zhang, D.-J. Guan, Off-line recognition of realistic Chinese handwriting using segmentation-free strategy. Pattern Recogn. **42**(1), 167–182 (2009)

T.-H. Su, T.-W. Zhang, H.-J. Huang, C.-L. Liu, Segmentation-free recognizer based on enhanced four plane feature for realistic Chinese handwriting, in *IEEE Conference on Pattern Recognition (ICPR)* (2008)

T.-H. Su, T.-W. Zhang, H.-J. Huang, Y. Zhou, HMM-based recognizer with segmentation-free strategy for unconstrained Chinese handwritten text, in *IEEE International Conference on Document Analysis and Recognition*, pp. 133–137 (2007b)

C.Y. Suen, M. Berthod, S. Mori, Automatic recognition of handprinted characters—the state of the art. Proc. IEEE **68**(4), 469–487 (1980)

C.Y. Suen, C. Nadal, R. Legault, T.A. Mai, L. Lam, Computer recognition of unconstrained handwritten numerals. Proc. IEEE **80**(7), 1162–1180 (1992)

Y.Y. Tang, C.Y. Suen, Document structures: a survey, in *Proceedings of the Second International Conference on Document Analysis and Recognition*, Tsukuba Science City, pp. 99–102 (1993)

G. Tauschek, Reading machine. US Patent 2026329, Dec 1935 (1929)

L.-T. Tu, Y.S. Lin, C.P. Yeh, I.S. Shyu, J.L. Wang, K.H. Joe, W.W. Lin, Recognition of handprinted Chinese characters by feature matching, in *Proceedings of the 1st National Workshop on Character Recognition*, pp. 166–175 (1991)

C. Viard-Gaudin, P.M. Lallican, S. Knerr, P. Binter, The IRESTE On/Off (IRONOFF) dual handwriting database, in *Proceedings of the 5th International Conference on Document Analysis and Recognition*, Bangalore, pp. 455–458 (1999)

A. Vinciarelli, S. Bengio, H. Bunke, Offline recognition of unconstrained handwritten texts using HMMs and statistical language models. IEEE Trans. Pattern Anal. Mach. Intell. **26**(6), 709–720 (2004)

T. Wakabayashi, S. Tsuruoka, F. Kimura, Y. Miyake, On the size and variable trans-formation of feature vector for handwritten character recognition. Trans. IEICE Jpn. **J76-D-II**(12), 2495–2503 (1993)

P. Wang, R. Shiau, Machine recognition of printed Chinese characters via transformation algorithms. Pattern Recogn. **5**(4), 303–321 (1973)

Q.-F. Wang, E. Cambria, C.-L. Liu, A. Hussain, Common sense knowledge for handwritten Chinese text recognition. Cogn. Comput. (2012a). doi:10.1007/s12559-012-9183-y

Q.-F. Wang, F. Yin, C.-L. Liu, Integrating language model in handwritten Chinese text recognition, in *International Conference on Document Analysis and Recognition*, pp. 1036–1040 (2009)

Q.-F. Wang, F. Yin, C.-L. Liu, Handwritten Chinese text recognition by integrating multiple contexts. IEEE Trans. Pattern Anal. Mach. Intell. 1469–1481 (2012b). doi:10.1109/TPAMI.2011.264

Q.R. Wang, C.Y. Suen, Analysis and design of a decision tree based on entropy reduction and its application to large character set recognition. IEEE Trans. Pattern Anal. Mach. Intell. **6**(4), 406–417 (1984)

Y. Wang, X. Ding, C. Liu, MQDF discriminative learning based offline handwritten Chinese character recognition, in *International Conference on Document Analysis and Recognition*, pp. 1100–1104 (2011a)

Y. Wang, X. Ding, C. Liu, MQDF retrained on selected sample set. IEICE Trans. **94-D**(10), 1933–1936 (2011b)

Y. Wang, Q. Huo, Sample-separation-margin based minimum classification error training of pattern classifiers with quadratic discriminant functions, in *IEEE International Conference on Acoustics, Speech and Signal Processing*, pp. 1866–1869 (2010)

Y. Wang, Q. Huo, Building compact recognizers of handwritten Chinese characters using precision constrained Gaussian model, minimum classification error training and parameter compression. IJDAR **14**(3), 255–262 (2011)

P.-K. Wong, C. Chan, Post-processing statistical language models for a handwritten Chinese character recognizer. IEEE Trans. Syst. Man Cybern. Part B **29**(2), 286–291 (1999)

Y. Wu, *Teaching computer to recognize characters—brief introduction to Chinese character recogntion* (Tsinghua University Press, Beijing, 2000). (in Chinese)

L. Xu, A. Krzyzak, C.Y. Suen, Methods for combining multiple classifiers and their applications to handwriting recognition. IEEE Trans. Syst. Man Cybern. **23**(3), 418–435 (1992)

L. Xu, F. Yin, Q.-F. Wang, C.-L. Liu, Touching character separation in chinese handwriting using visibility-based foreground analysis, in *ICDAR*, pp. 859–863 (2011)

J. Xue, X. Ding, C. Liu, R. Zhang, W. Qian, Location and interpretation of destination addresses on handwritten Chinese envelopes. Pattern Recogn. Lett. **22**(6), 639–656 (2001)

H. Yamada, Contour DP matching method and its application to handprinted Chinese character recognition, in *Proceedings of 7th International Conference on Pattern Recognition*, pp. 389–392 (1984)

H. Yamada, T. Saito, S. Mori, An improvement of correlation method—shift similarity. J. IECE Jpn. **J64-D**, 970–976 (1981)

K. Yamamoto, Recognition of handprinted Kanji characters by relaxation matching. J. IECE Jpn. **J65-D**, 1167–1174 (1982)

S. Yamamoto, A. Nakajima, K. Nakata, Chinese character recognition by hierarchical pattern matching, in *International Conference on Pattern Recognition*, pp. 187–196 (1973)

Y. Yao, Handprinted Chinese character recognition via neural networks. Pattern Recogn. Lett. **7**(1), 19–25 (1988)

M. Yasuda, H. Fujisawa, An improved correlation method for character recognition. Syst. Comput. Controls **10**(2), 29–38 (1979)

M. Yasuda, K. Yamamoto, H. Yamada, T. Saito, An improved correlation method for character recognition in a reciprocal feature field. IECE Trans. **J68-D**(3), 353–360 (1985)

F. Yin, Q.-F. Wang, C.-L. Liu, Integrating geometric context for text alignment of handwritten Chinese documents, in *ICFHR*, pp. 7–12 (2010)

M. Yoshida, M. Eden, Handwritten Chinese character recognition by an analysis-by-synthesis method, in *International Conference on Pattern Recognition*, pp. 197–204 (1973)

H. Zhang, J. Guo, Introduction to HCL2000 database, in *Proceedings of Sino-Japan Symposium on Intelligent Information Networks*, Beijing (2000)

S. Zhao, Z. Chi, P. Shi, H. Yan, Two-stage segmentation of unconstrained handwritten Chinese characters. Pattern Recogn. **36**(1), 145–156 (2003)

S. Zhou, Q. Chen, X. Wang, HIT-OR3C: an opening recognition corpus for Chinese characters, in *Proceedings of the 9th IAPR International Workshop on Document Analysis Systems* (2010)

X.-D. Zhou, C.-L. Liu, M. Nakagawa, Online handwritten Japanese character string recognition using conditional random fields, in *ICDAR*, pp. 521–525 (2009)

X.-D. Zhou, J.-L. Yu, C.-L. Liu, T. Nagasaki, K. Marukawa, Online handwritten Japanese character string recognition incorporating geometric context, in *ICDAR*, pp. 48–52 (2007)

G.K. Zipf, *Human Behavior and the Principle of Least Effort* (Addison-Wesley, Cambridge, 1949)

M.J. Zobrak, A method for rapid recognition hand drawn line patterns. Ms thesis, University of Pittsburgh, Pennsylvania, 1966

Y. Zou, K. Yu, K. Wang, Continuous Chinese handwriting recognition with language model, in *11th International Conference on Frontiers in Handwriting Recognition*, pp. 344–348 (2008)

Chapter 2
HIT-MW Database

Abstract Standard databases play a fundamental part in handwriting recognition research. This chapter presents a Chinese handwriting database named HIT-MW, designed to facilitate Chinese handwritten text recognition. Both the writers and the texts for handcopying are carefully sampled using a systematic approach. To collect naturally written handwriting, the forms were distributed by postal mail or middleman instead of face to face. The current version of HIT-MW includes 853 forms and 1,86,444 characters that were produced under natural and unconstrained conditions without preprinted character boxes. The statistics show that the database provides an excellent representation of the realistic Chinese handwriting. Many new applications concerning realistic handwriting recognition can be supported by the database. Hundreds of institutes and universities have begun using the HIT-MW database in their experiments over the world.

2.1 Introduction

Standard databases play fundamental roles in handwriting recognition research. On the one hand, they provide a large number of training and testing data, resulting in high model fit and reliable confidence in statistic. On the other hand, they offer a means by which evaluation among different recognition algorithms can be performed. More and more handwriting researchers begin to pay much attention to the database standardization and evaluate their work using standard databases.

Dozens of handwriting databases were released in literature for handwriting recognition before 2006. We tabulate some of them in Table 2.1. From the table, we just highlight the following two insights. First, English handwriting recognition is one of the most thoroughly studied branches not only in recognition strategy but also in database standardization. There are three different recognition strategies to

T. Su, *Chinese Handwriting Recognition: An Algorithmic Perspective*,   23
SpringerBriefs in Electrical and Computer Engineering,
DOI: 10.1007/978-3-642-31812-2_2, © The Author(s) 2013

Table 2.1 Standard databases for handwriting recognition

Database	Language	Scope	Years	Source
Highleyman	English	Alphanum	1961	Highleyman (1961)
Munson		Alphanum	1968	Munson (1968)
Suen		Numeral	1972	Suen et al. (1980)
CENPARMI		Postcode	1992	Suen et al. (1992)
CEDAR		City name	1994	Hull (1994)
CAMBRIDGE		Sentence	1994	Senior and Robinson (1998)
UNIPEN		Alphanum, Word, Sentence	1994	Guyon et al. (1994)
IAM		Sentence	1998	v1 (Marti and Bunke 1999) v2 (Marti and Bunke 2002)
IAAS-4M	Chinese	Character	1985	Liu et al. (1989)
THOCR-HCD		Character	~1985	Fu et al. (2008)
ITRI		Character	1991	Tu et al. (1991)
SCUT-IRAC		Character	1996	Jin (1996)
HCL2000		Character	2000	Zhang and Guo (2000)
HK2002		Character	2002	Ge et al. (2002)
ETL-8	Japanese	Character	1976	Mori et al. (1979)
ETL-9		Character	1985	Saito et al. (1985)
TUAT		Character	1997	Nakagawa et al. (1997)
PE92	Korean	Character	1992	Kim et al. (1996)
KU-1		Character	2000	Park et al. (2000)
IRONOFF	French	Character	1999	Viard-Gaudin et al. (1999)
GRUHD	Greek	Character	2000	Kavallieratou et al. (2001)
ISI	Indian	Alphanum	2005	Bhattacharya and Chaudhuri (2005)

English handwriting: segmentation-based recognition, segmentation-free recognition, and holistic recognition (Casey and Lecolinet 1996). When arranging the English handwritten databases chronologically, we find that the handwritten scope has transmitted from digit or letter (Highleyman 1961; Munson 1968; Suen et al. 1980, 1992) to city name (Hull 1994) or words (Guyon et al. 1994), further to sentence (Senior and Robinson 1998; Marti and Bunke 1999, 2002; Guyon et al. 1994) and that application fields have expanded from small lexicon domains, such as bank check reading (Guillevic and Suen 1998) and address recognition (Yacoubi et al. 2002), to large lexicon and general unconstrained domains (Kim et al. 1999; Vinciarelli et al. 2004; Zimmermann and Bunke 2004).

Second, nine databases were mentioned in literature for Chinese or Kanji character recognition before 2006, namely ETL-8/ETL-9 (Mori et al. 1979; Saito et al. 1985), IAAS-4M (Liu et al. 1989), THOCR-HCD (Fu et al. 2008), ITRI (Tu et al. 1991), SCUT-IRAC (Jin 1996), TUAT (Nakagawa et al. 1997), HCL2000 (Zhang and Guo 2000), and HK2002 (Ge et al. 2002) and all of them follow the same paradigm: each participant is requested to write a large set of Chinese characters [commonly 3,755 characters in the First Level GB2312-1980 (General Administration of Technology of the People's Republic of China 1980)], and each character should be carefully written within a preprinted character box. As a result, each character class contains the same number of samples, no matter whether it is rarely or frequently used in daily life. Meanwhile, samples in those databases are far from real-world ones, given that they are handprinted within character boxes. In real-world applications, the input to handwriting reader is multiple lines of handwritten text even running up and down or with outliers (for instance, crossing off a character/word with special marks), instead of isolated characters. So, not only character recognition, but the text line segmentation, outlier modeling, and linguistic constraint are needed in real-world handwriting recognition. Moreover, since these databases are character-level, the recognition must be performed after explicit character segmentation. Just as Sayre's paradox (Sayre 1973) goes, segmentation is prone to error and difficult to make correction afterward. Generally, much of the error rate can be attributed to imperfect segmentation. In addition, there are not enough data to support segmentation experiments, since the standard Chinese databases include only characters. As a tradeoff, such experiments are conducted on Chinese mail addresses (Liu et al. 2002), though the number of them is limited. Indeed, a large handwritten Chinese text-level database is in great need.

We have motivated to study the general purpose Chinese handwriting recognition. After 3 years work, we compiled HIT-MW (HIT is the abbreviation of Harbin Institute of Technology, and MW means it is written by Multiple Writers), a handwritten Chinese text database for the first time. Comparing to CAM-BRIDGE and IAM, our database has at least three distinctions. First, the handwriting is naturally written with no rulers that can be used to make the text line straight by and large. This feature makes it suitable for conducting experiments on Chinese text line segmentation. Second, the underlying texts for handcopying are sampled from People's Daily corpus in a systematic way and the writers are carefully chosen to give a balanced distribution. Third, it is collected by mail or middleman instead of face to face, resulting in some real handwriting phenomena, such as miswriting and erasing. Besides text line segmentation, the HIT-MW is fit to research segmentation-free recognition algorithms, to verify the effect of statistical language model (SLM) in real handwriting situation, and to study the nerve mechanism of Chinese handcopying activity.

With the HIT-MW database, the recognition scope has shifted to the unconstrained Chinese handwriting. Chinese researchers can set out to overcome the barrier associated with the practical reading machine for Chinese handwriting. Inspired by HIT-MW database, another three Chinese handwriting databases are built recently: SCUT-COUCH (Jin et al. 2011), HIT-OR3C (Zhou et al. 2010) and CASIA-OLHDB/CASIA-HWDB (Liu et al. 2011). Among them, HIT-MW database and CASIA-HWDB can facilitate the off-line tasks while others can support the online tasks. Provided with these training samples, sophisticated learning algorithms can be investigated.

This chapter presents the overall process for creation of HIT-MW database. The flowchart of developing HIT-MW is illustrated in Fig. 2.1. The next section describes the sampling strategy. Then the handwriting collection and handwriting

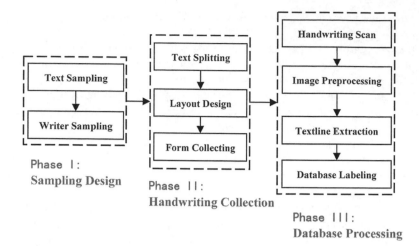

Fig. 2.1 Flowchart of HIT-MW database

processing are discussed in Sects. 2.3 and 2.4, respectively. Section 2.5 first analyzes the basic statistics of the database to verify the effectiveness of our sampling strategy, and then presents two real handwriting phenomena, i.e., miswriting and erasing. Potential applications of our database are explored in Sect. 2.6. Finally, discussions and concluding remarks are given in Sect. 2.7.

2.2 Sampling Strategy

Our database is to make a reasonable representation of the realistic Chinese handwriting, so it is important to carefully design sampling schemes. In this section, we describe two sampling schemes, dealing with objective writers and electronic data, respectively.

2.2.1 Writer Sampling

We determine our potential users to be college students, government clerk graduated from university, and senior students in high school who will be potential college students in the next year. There are three reasons. First, according to the handwriting theory, the handwriting goes into a stable and consistent state at 25 years old, and after that there is little change. Second, the college students are enrolled throughout the country, so the handwriting by them can be seen as samples from the whole country. This diminishes the sampling bias to some degree. Third, it is mainly the well-educated people who are potential users of handwriting recognition in China, such as personal notes and manuscripts transcription.

Due to special users oriented, we need not sample the writers randomly. Instead, we divide the country into three regions, i.e., north region, middle region, and south region, and select one city handy from each region. Just using this simple sampling method, we obtain balanced writer samples (Cf. Sect. 2.5).

2.2.2 Text Sampling

We choose People's Daily corpus as the data source of our database. In the natural language processing field, People's Daily is extensively used as Chinese written language corpus, covering comprehensive topics such as politics, economics, science and technology, and culture. Using corpus as our data source instead of chaotic electronic texts demonstrates three advantages: linguistic context is automatically built in; Database can be easily expanded with tremendous texts to sample from; More frequently a character occurs, more training samples it possesses. Thereby, our database can be collected in a progressive way and is helpful to conduct the linguistic post-processing after the recognition stage.

We sample texts with a stratified random manner. To reserve more data for future expansion, we only use texts of the People's Daily 2004 (news ranging from January to October is chosen at this stage). We first divide texts into ten groups according to month. Then we randomly draw 25 texts without replacement from each group. Using this method, we obtain a compact and sound approximation to Chinese written language (the verification is put aside in Sect. 2.5).

2.3 Database Acquisition

Once the texts are extracted, we start the collection process. Initially, we split each text into smaller and manageable segments. After several trials, we make each of them about 200 characters consisting of a few complete sentences. Next, we format them into a clear and uniform layout. To design an informative layout, some considerations have been taken. Whenever all those have been done, we distribute forms to writers. Finally, we select forms according to special criteria.

2.3.1 Text Partition

Texts previously sampled from corpus should be split into smaller segments. The number of characters in texts ranges from tens to thousands, which is inconvenient to distribute. In order to split each of them into a series of reasonable-size text segments, we consider the following two factors. First, it is wise to avoid breaking each complete sentence, in which as much linguistic context as possible can be held. Some punctuation marks—the period, the exclamation mark, the question mark, and combination of them with quotation marks—serve as sentence end. Others, such as the semicolon, the dash, and ellipsis mark can also be selected as sentence end if necessary.

Second, segment should have a reasonable number of characters. If it is too short, the writer's style and handwriting variability are hardly obtained. In the opposite case, it makes the writer's hand-muscle and vision muscle tired, which in turn mostly makes the handwriting illegible. Moreover, we will not collect the handwriting completely when big-size characters are presented.

Based on these two factors, we conduct simulated experiments several times. It seems that segments between 50 and 400 characters are acceptable. Further discussion is presented in the next subsection.

2.3.2 Layout Design

When we print text segments as forms, it is the layout that serves as an interface to writers. It is a nontrivial task to make it friendly and informative. The design of layout follows three criteria. First, the layout is simple and clear. Each form is divided into three distinct blocks: guideline block, text block, and writing block. The horizontal lines are used to separate the adjacent blocks and the faces of font to discern different information within block.

Second, we compress the writing guidelines to give more space reserved for handwriting. We make our commands concise by using short phrases and arrange them within five text lines with small font.

Third, we make use of implicit restrictions. In some cases, we want the writer to follow a special pattern, but it has difficulties to express in words. For example, we expect that the handwriting has a relatively small skew angle, but if we express it as a command, it will make the writer too careful to write naturally. Then we use horizontal lines both at top and bottom as references. It can help the writer know whether his handwriting is skew or not, and make some remedies to reduce the skew adaptively (In our opinion, totally freedom without any restrictions in handwriting collection is intractable).

After several recursions of feedback and modification, the final layout is illustrated in Fig. 2.2 (the writing block shown here is scaled down vertically to make the graph smaller). Each form is identified by a 4-pair digit code and each pair stands for certain meaning, e.g., 04090902 means that it is the second text segment of the ninth text sampled from September 2004.

样本编号：04090902   此手写样本授予哈尔滨工业大学文字识别研究之用

性别 男□女□ 年龄   职业   签名

书写要求：

保持纸张勿折、正反面均清洁，规范书写、勿潦草，蓝、黑或蓝黑色笔均可，尽量少连笔少涂污，行间留出空隙。
请抄写下面的印刷文本到空白区内，谢谢您的合作！

　　郑培民生前是中共湖南省委副书记、湖南省人大常委会副主任，2002年3月11日因心脏病突发，牺牲在工作岗位上。2003年3月11日，中共中央总书记胡锦涛作出重要批示，号召向郑培民同志学习。2004年3月，潇湘电影集团、中国电影集团和大成公司投拍影片《郑培民》，并于国庆前夕奉献给全国观众。

　　该片取材于郑培民同志生前的生活小事，以修建公路为主线，集中体现了他权为民所用、情为民所系、利为民所谋的情怀，成功地塑造了一个党的好干部的典型形象。

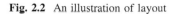

Fig. 2.2 An illustration of layout

2.3.3 Form Collection

Forms are distributed by mail or middleman instead of face to face. This makes the writers impossible to tailor the handwriting for easy recognition, not exactly knowing for what their handwriting will be used. Naturally written handwriting is more likely to acquire.

   Once a pile of handwriting forms are collected, we accept the legible ones, and the illegible or lost ones are reprinted and distributed again. Handwriting is thought as legible, if it runs from left to right, its contents are what we have appointed (a little miswriting and erasing are allowed), and a majority of it can be read correctly by human.

2.4 Database Processing

The accepted handwriting is scanned into computer as digital image and then pixel-level processing is applied on it. The processing includes frame eliminating and binarization to give a clean and compact registration of the handwriting. Next, we transcribe the handwriting's ground truth that will serve as standard answers when calculating the recognition rate. Eventually, the database is ready for segmentation-free recognition by separating the text lines.

2.4.1 Handwriting Digitalization

Each writing block of legible forms is scanned into computer by Microtek ScanMaker 4180. The resolution is set to 300 dpi. Images are saved as gray-scale BMP files with no compression and named after their forms' code. The average storage space of each image is about 2.1 M bytes.

2.4.2 Image Preprocessing

We perform image preprocessing on each scanned image. First, we eliminate the frame lines enclosing the writing block. We deal with them in an automatic way, and manually eliminate them once the lines are off standard positions. We pay special attention to preserve the smoothness of its strokes intersecting the frame lines. Then, we binarize handwriting image using Otsu algorithm (Otsu 1979). The binary image is named after the grayscale image and a letter "b" is inserted as the prefix. The black and white version of the handwriting image named 04090902 is shown in Fig. 2.3.

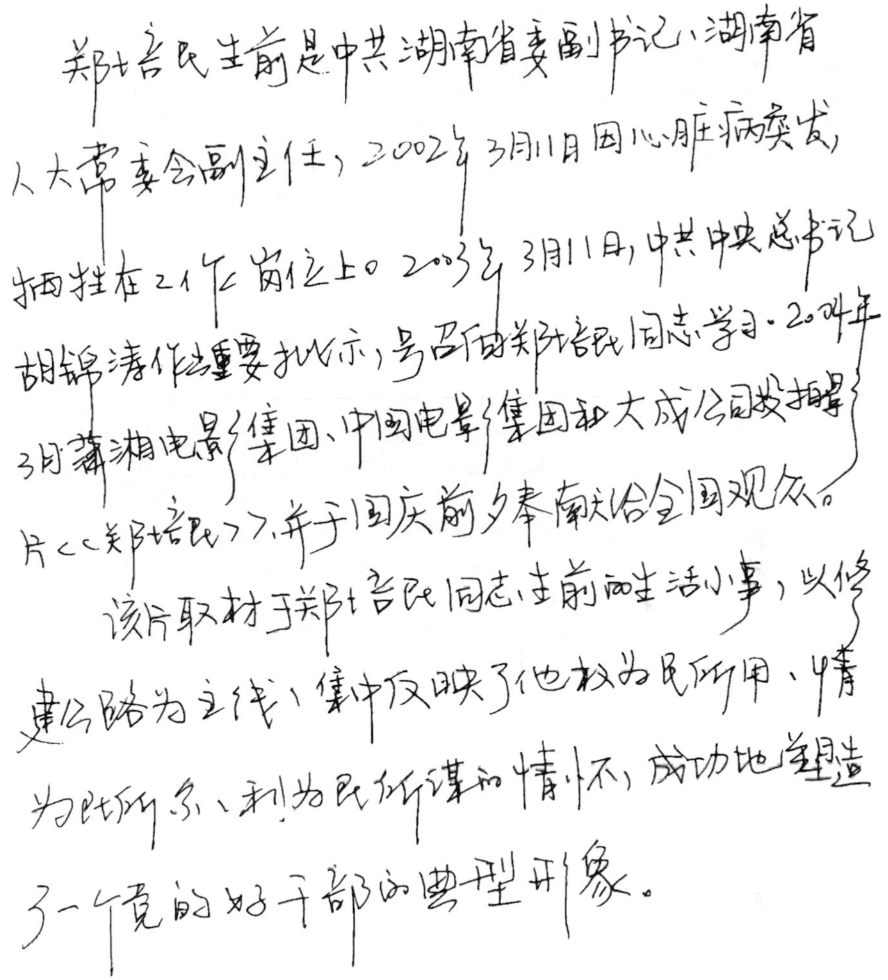

Fig. 2.3 Binary image of a handwritten sample named 04090902. © (2007) IEEE. Reprinted, with permission, from Ref. Su et al. (2007b)

2.4.3 Database Labeling

The ground truth acts as the standard answers to the handwriting image. To evaluate the performance, transcription from recognition engine is compared with the ground truth. That is to say, labeling the database to generate its ground truth is the preliminary stage for the development of the recognition system. Generating the ground truth file involves two different level alignments: a text line level alignment and a character level alignment. The former makes text segment produce a new line which corresponds to the end of each handwriting text line. The latter crosses off the deleted characters from each segment, key in the inserted

Fig. 2.4 The ground truth on document level of Fig. 2.3. Reprinted from Ref. Su et al. (2007a), with kind permission from Springer Science + Business Media

郑培民生前是中共湖南省委副书记、湖南省
人大常委会副主任，2002年3月11日因心脏病突发，
牺牲在工作岗位上。2003年3月11日，中共中央总书记
胡锦涛作出重要批示，号召向郑培民同志学习。2004年
3月，潇湘电影集团、中国电影集团和大成公司投拍影
片《郑培民》，并于国庆前夕奉献给全国观众。
该片取材于郑培民同志生前的生活小事，以修
建公路为主线，集中反映了他权为民所用、情
为民所系、利为民所谋的情怀，成功地塑造
了一个党的好干部的典型形象。

characters and modify the substituted characters. An example of the labeled ground truth on document level is illustrated in Fig. 2.4. Further, each row of the text is extracted and saved as a separate file (ground truth on text line level).

For the segmentation-free recognition systems, there is no need to annotate character boundaries, while the segmentation-based or integrated segmentation-recognition systems must provide character level alignment. A recognition-based ground truthing tool is employed to annotate the HIT-MW database (Yin et al. 2009). An annotated segment is shown in Fig. 2.5.

2.4.4 Text Line Extraction

Many skewed handwritten documents even with strokes touching and overlapping between adjacent text lines are presented in HIT-MW database (as shown in Fig. 2.3). We have developed a fast skew correction algorithm to improve the recall rate of text lines.

Each Chinese character can be decomposed into a group of strokes. Those strokes fall into four basic patterns: horizontal stroke, vertical stroke, left-falling stroke, and right-falling stroke. In GB2312-1980, the national encoding standard used in China, each Chinese character consists of about 15.17 basic strokes and horizontal strokes account for 39.51 % of them (Wu and Ding 1992). In other words, there are on average six horizontal strokes in a Chinese character. In addition, about 99.8 % of characters in GB2312-1980 include horizontal strokes. Those statistics mean that horizontal strokes are stable features in Chinese characters.

We employ the angular histogram of the horizontal strokes. Since they encode rich information of horizontal strokes, we incorporate them into projection profile to estimate the skew angles of handwritten documents from HIT-MW database in a fast and robust way.

We calculate the horizontal run-length of each document and only keep the strokes whose run-length is greater than T_s, where T_s is a threshold relating to the

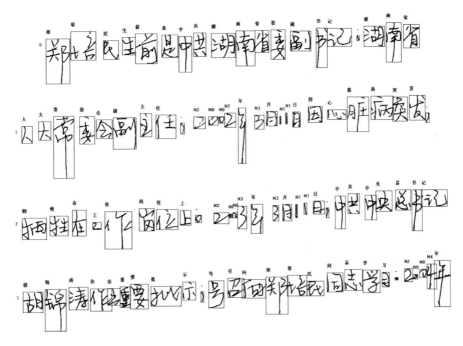

Fig. 2.5 An annotated segment in character level

Fig. 2.6 Horizontal run-length histogram of HIT-MW database. The curve is interpolated by cubic spline. © (2007) IEEE. Reprinted, with permission, from Ref. Su et al. (2007b)

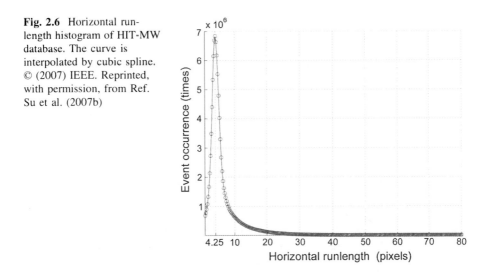

average stroke width (ASW). The value of ASW is estimated from horizontal run-length histogram. Figure 2.6 illustrates the run-length histogram of HIT-MW database. The curve is smoothed by cubic spline. We set ASW as the runlength with maximum peak. From the curve, we can see that ASW is about 4.25 pixels.

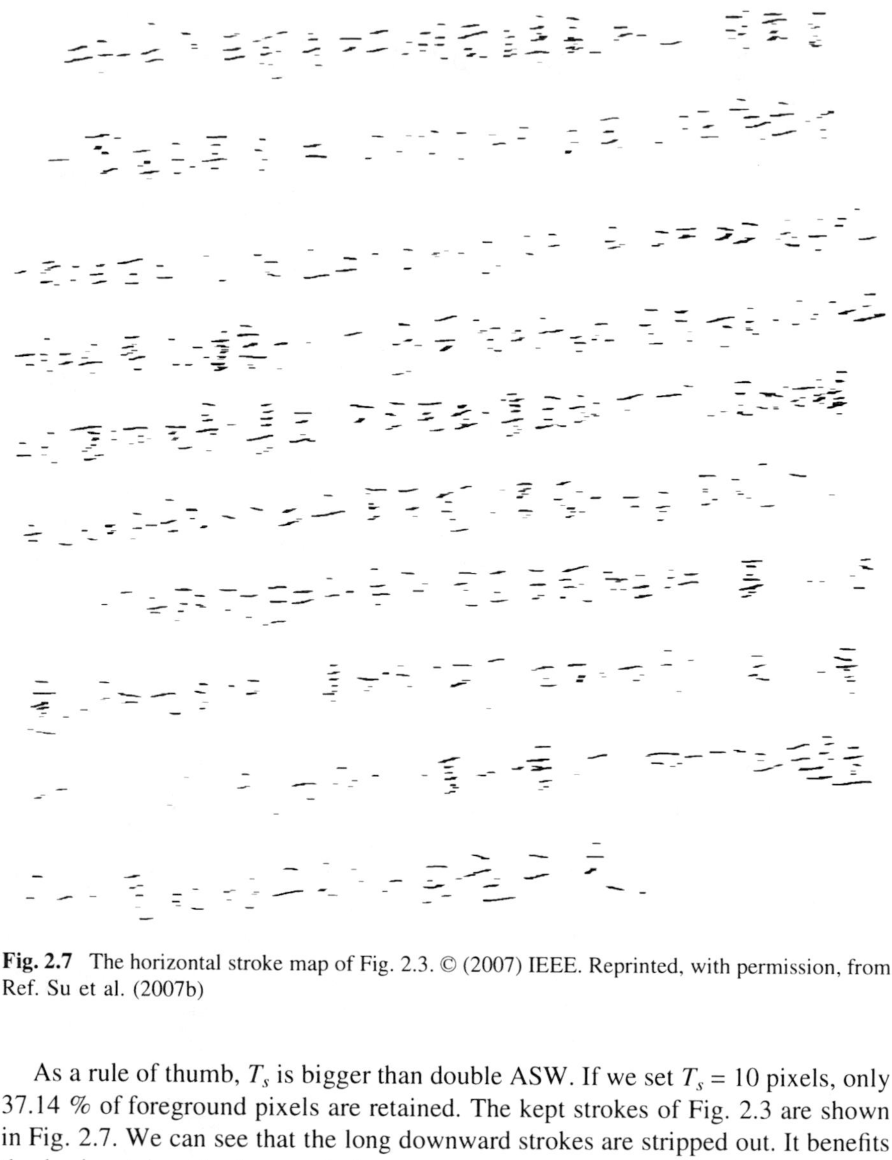

Fig. 2.7 The horizontal stroke map of Fig. 2.3. © (2007) IEEE. Reprinted, with permission, from Ref. Su et al. (2007b)

As a rule of thumb, T_s is bigger than double ASW. If we set $T_s = 10$ pixels, only 37.14 % of foreground pixels are retained. The kept strokes of Fig. 2.3 are shown in Fig. 2.7. We can see that the long downward strokes are stripped out. It benefits the horizontal projection analysis as it presents more acute transitions between peaks and valleys. In addition, small noise can be discarded with ease.

Further, we extract the center point of each remaining stroke and we call it representative point. This step discards at least nine-tenth foreground pixels of above horizontal strokes. In total, more than 96 % foreground pixels are discarded and the bias from long pseudo-strokes is reduced greatly. Figure 2.8 shows the center point version of Fig. 2.7.

The skew detection can be modeled as a classification problem and the skew angle of a document can be identified as the class maximizing a cost function as follows:

Fig. 2.8 The representative points of Fig. 2.7, where each point is expanded nine times to give a clear view. © (2007) IEEE. Reprinted, with permission, from Ref. Su et al. (2007b)

$$\theta' = \arg\max_{\theta} \Omega_\theta. \tag{2.1}$$

The cost function defines as a weighted sum of three terms, has the following form:

$$\Omega_\theta = a_1 \sigma_\theta + a_2 \phi_\theta + a_3 \varpi_\theta, \tag{2.2}$$

where σ_θ refers to the variance of the horizontal projection histogram, ϕ_θ the total gaps (the number of positions with zero histogram value) divided by document height, and ϖ_θ the normalized maximum of the histogram. The weights, a_is' are determined from experiments.

Fig. 2.9 Curves of Ω_θ for Fig. 2.3 based on whole document, horizontal strokes, and representative points respectively when $\theta \in [-5,5]$. The maximum of each curve corresponds to the estimated skew angle. © (2007) IEEE. Reprinted, with permission, from Ref. Su et al. (2007b)

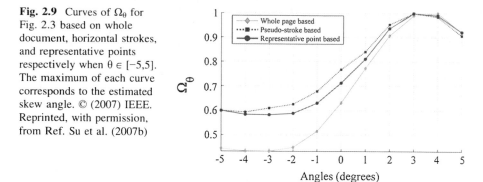

The cost function curves for Fig. 2.3 based on the whole document, horizontal strokes, and representative points respectively are plotted in Fig. 2.9 with $a_1 = 1$ (the variances in the figure are normalized to one to put those curves into the same axis). From the figure, the angular projection of representative points has a comparative ability with that of horizontal strokes to extract the right skew angle. The decision by the angular projection of whole document is one degree off the right angle.

Now we show the range of skew angles which can be addressed by our method. A horizontal stroke can be modeled as a rectangle and we define: l is the width of the stroke, h the height of the stroke, γ the acute angle between the diagonal and horizontal direction, and α the skew angle of the stroke.

Commonly l is bigger than T_s. Due to the value of α, three cases can be reached:

(1) If $\alpha < \gamma$, the longest horizontal runlength is bigger than l and the horizontal stroke can be located (as in Fig. 2.10a);
(2) If $\alpha = \gamma$, the longest horizontal runlength is l and the horizontal stroke can also be located (see Fig. 2.10b);
(3) If $\alpha > \gamma$, the problem becomes a little complex. The longest horizontal runlength is $h/\sin\alpha$. Thus the relationships between T_s and $h/\sin\alpha$ determinate whether the horizontal stroke can be located. When $h/\sin\alpha$ is bigger than or equal to T_s, the horizontal stroke can be located (showed in Fig. 2.10c); otherwise, it will be lost (shown in Fig. 2.10d).

Specifically, the maximum of skew angle should be smaller than 25 degrees when: $T_s = 10$, $h = 4.25$, and $l > 10$. By carefully tuning the ratio between h and T_s, we can determine the range of skew angles to be examined.

After the skew correction, the recall rate of the text lines by global horizontal projection is improved by 17.09 %, as indicated in Table 2.2. Three out of ten text lines of the handwriting in Fig. 2.3 can be successfully recalled by global projection following the skew correction (as in Fig. 2.11a, c, d).

In order to handle the complex text lines (just as in Fig. 2.11b), we adapt the genetic algorithm-based HIDER method (Su et al. 2008) to find the failure blocks (those cannot successfully separated by partial projection) and then heuristic-based thinning algorithm [similar to (Liang and Shi 2005)] will be used to extract the text

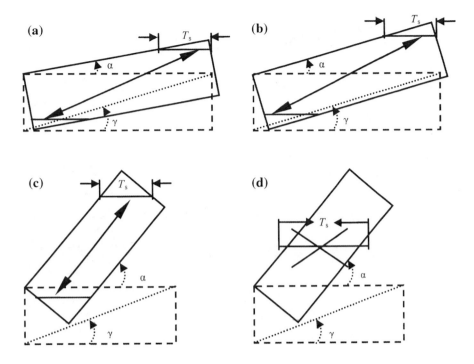

Fig. 2.10 A horizontal stroke with a skew of α will be located (a-c) and lost (d). The arrow indicates the zone containing horizontal runlength bigger than T_s. © [2007] IEEE. Reprinted, with permission, from Ref. Su et al. (2007b). **a** $\alpha < \gamma$ **b** $\alpha = \gamma$, **c** $\alpha > \gamma$, $h/\sin\alpha \geq T_s$ **d** $\alpha > \gamma$, $h/\sin\alpha < T_s$

Table 2.2 The number of recalled text lines (recall rate) in two setups

No skew correction	With skew correction
4062 (51.92 %)	5394 (69.01 %)

© (2007) IEEE. Reprinted with correction, with permission, from Ref. Su et al. (2007b)

border lines. As a key preprocessing step for Chinese handwriting recognition, following researchers have studied the text line segmentation problem from different perspectives and steady progress can be observed (Yin and Liu 2009a, b; Koo and Cho 2012).

2.5 Database Statistics

The HIT-MW database is the first collection of Chinese handwritten texts in handwriting recognition domain. More than 780 participants produce their handwriting naturally. In this section we will present HIT-MW's features by a data-driven way. First, we describe the basic statistics, which show sound writer

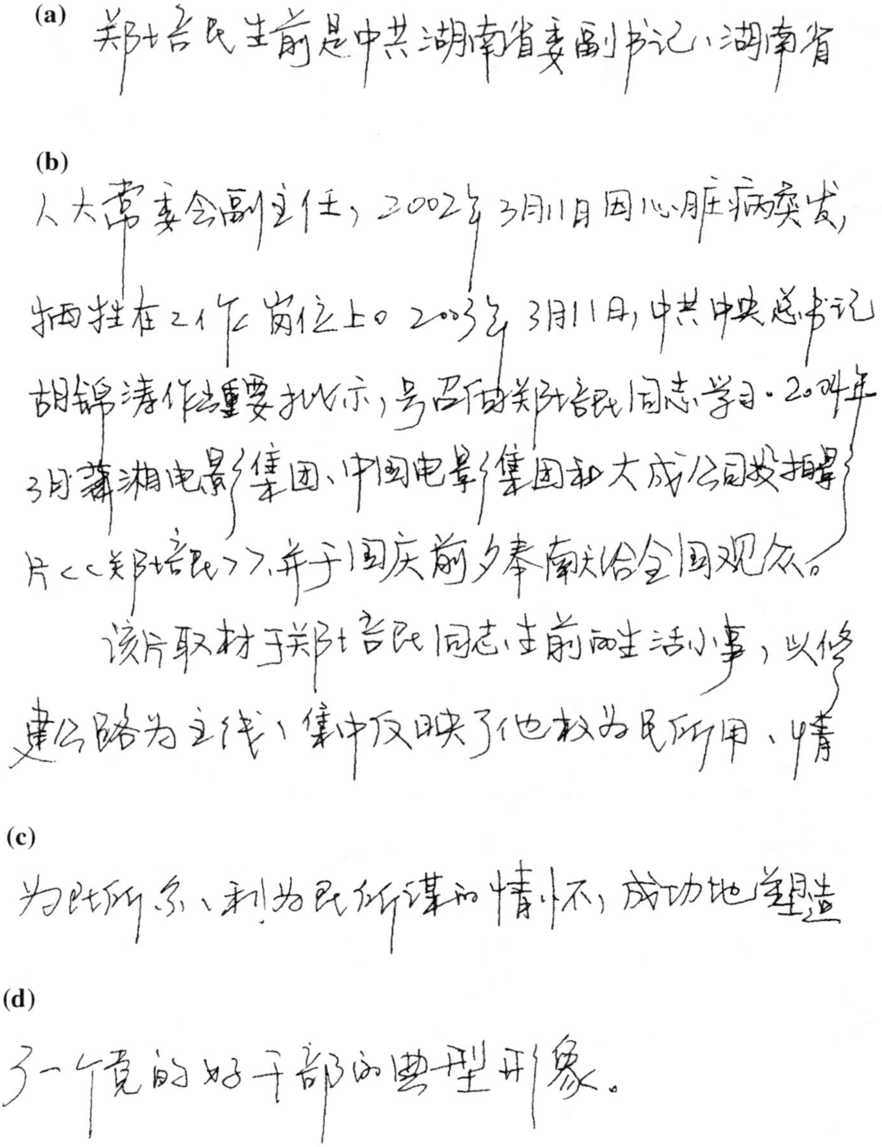

(a) 郑培民生前是中共湖南省委副书记、湖南省

(b) 人大常委会副主任，2002年3月11日因心脏病突发，牺牲在工作岗位上。2003年3月11日，中共中央总书记胡锦涛作出重要批示，号召向郑培民同志学习。2004年3月潇湘电影集团、中国电影集团和大成公司发把影片《《郑培民》》，并于国庆前夕奉献给全国观众。

该片取材于郑培民同志生前的生活小事，以修建公路为主线、集中反映了他权为民所用、情

(c) 为比所系、利为民所谋的情怀，成功地塑造

(d) 了一个党的好干部的典型形象。

Fig. 2.11 The segmentation result by global projection after skew correction. Reprinted from Ref. Su et al. (2007a), with kind permission from Springer Science + Business Media. **a** The first text line is extracted successfully, **b** The second part is failed to segment, **c** The second to last text line is extracted successfully, **d** The last text line is extracted successfully

Table 2.3 Lexicon of HIT-MW database versus GB2312-1980 character set (unit: characters)

Within GBset				Beyond GBset
flGBset	slGBset	ASCII	Others	
2746	215	48	27	5

Reprinted from Ref. Su et al. (2007a), with kind permission from Springer Science + Business Media

distributions and an appealing lexical coverage on the People's Daily corpus. Next, we focus our attention on two key handwriting phenomena, i.e., miswriting and erasing, and analyze them, respectively.

2.5.1 Basic Statistics

We have collected 853 legible Chinese handwriting samples. There are 1,86,444 characters in total including letters, punctuations besides Chinese characters, and these characters lead to 8,664 text lines. By simple computation, we get the following statistics: Each sample has 10.16 text lines; each text line has 21.51 characters; each sample includes 218.57 characters.

Mining the ground truth files of our database, we derive following results. The lexicon of the database has 3,041 entries. In other words, on average each character occurs 61.31 times. Most of the entries fall into GB2312-1980 character set (hereafter, abbreviated as GBset), and details are summarized in Table 2.3. Chinese handwritten character databases (such as HCL2000, IAAS-4M) only consist of the first level Chinese characters of GBset (flGBset in short, and similarly slGBset for the second level Chinese characters of GBset). Unlike them, our database samples characters by their real use in daily life. As a result, not only most of flGBset but a quantity of slGBset are included (even several characters beyond GBset are included).

Moreover, to check its representative capability, we plot its coverage over People's Daily corpus with 7,95,09,778 characters in Fig. 2.12. Note that, the corpus has already excluded the data of People's Daily 2004 to give objective coverage estimation. From the graph, we can see that a 1,800 character lexicon covers 97.60 % of the corpus, and the full-size lexicon 99.33 % of the corpus. The lexicon is extracted from the database according to the character frequency. For example, a 100 character lexicon consists of 100 most frequently occurred characters in the database.

In another way, we plot the scatter map in Fig. 2.13 between lexicon of database and that of corpus. Each dot in the figure, (x, y), means that a character

Fig. 2.12 Lexicon size of HIT-MW versus coverage of people's daily corpus. Reprinted from Ref. Su et al. (2007a), with kind permission from Springer Science + Business Media

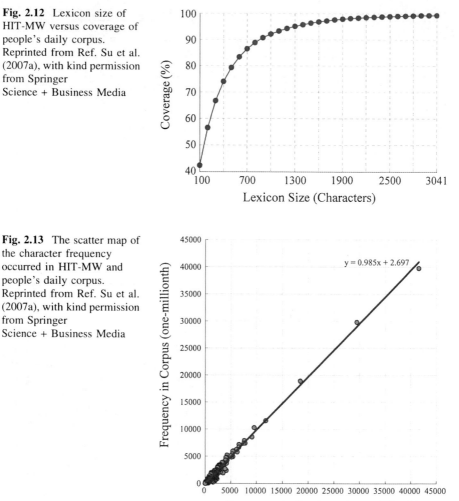

Fig. 2.13 The scatter map of the character frequency occurred in HIT-MW and people's daily corpus. Reprinted from Ref. Su et al. (2007a), with kind permission from Springer Science + Business Media

appears x times in database and y times in corpus. We can see from the figure that the cloud of dots is mainly spread along the auxiliary diagonal. Minimizing the least squares, we obtain a regression line as follow:

$$y = 0.9853x + 2.6973. \tag{2.3}$$

We can see that the x value is approximately the same of y. By correlation analysis, we get a high coefficient of 0.9936 (the number of dots is 3,037).

Further, we calculate the writer's distribution. We mark the three sampled cities as City A, City B, and City C, respectively. From the view of city distribution in Fig. 2.14, the sampled writers are mainly from City A with a proportion of 67 %. Seen from Table 2.4, the department distribution of writers is near to that

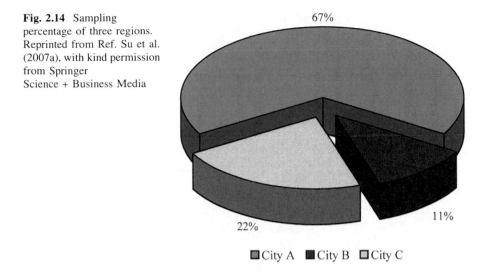

Fig. 2.14 Sampling percentage of three regions. Reprinted from Ref. Su et al. (2007a), with kind permission from Springer Science + Business Media

calculated from real data of college students of 2004 (National Bureau of Statistics of China 2005). Similarly, Table 2.5 shows that the sex distribution of our database has a good coincidence with that calculated from real educational statistics of 1998 (Ministry of Education 1998).

In summary, both the distribution of writer and the coverage of lexical entry show the effectiveness of the proposed sampling schemes.

2.5.2   Erasing Statistics

The handcopying activity relates three interactive processes. Initially, the vision perceives the stimuli and transmits them as signals to the brain. Then, the brain stores the information in memory. And as the last step, the brain makes certain muscles active and further those muscles drive the writing instrument to run on the paper. Errors in any process will result in erasing or miswriting. For example, there is an erasure marked by a black dot at the eighth character of the last line in Fig. 2.15.

We group erasures by erasing mark and month in Table 2.6. In real handwriting, writers use erasing marks to express the marked character is discarded. To different persons, their marks may vary in some way, for example, writer A may use a double slash (//), while writer B uses a black dot (•). From Table 2.6, we can learn some points. First, erasures are common in our database. There are 382 instances of erasure totally, and about one instance appears out of every two handwriting samples. If we do not model it properly in recognition stage, it may decrease the recognition rate by 0.20 % solely. Moreover, when SLM is used as postprocessing, it may make things worse. As an extreme, if the recognition is based on segmentation-free strategy, about 4.39 % of the characters will be under threat.

Table 2.4 Writers from science and engineering departments versus college students of 2004 from that reprinted from Ref. Su et al. (2007a), with kind permission from Springer Science + Business Media

Of 2004	Sampled
61.37 %	60.69 %

Table 2.5 Gender distribution comparison between writers sampled and students of year 1998

Boy writers sampled		Boy students of 1998	
High school	University	High school	University
57.25 %	62.54 %	57.26 %	63.29 %

Reprinted from Ref. Su et al. (2007a), with kind permission from Springer Science + Business Media

建行主要业务指标.

创历史同期最高水平.

本报北京2月12日讯,记者田俊荣报道:中国建设银行行长张恩照.
在近日召开的2004年建设工作会议上说,过去一年是建行向现代金融企业
转变的重要一年,各项业务不仅呈现出强劲的发展势头,而且资产质量
和经营效益也得到进一步提高,主要业务指标再创历史同期最高水
平.全行境内外业务实现拨备前利润512.3亿元,其中境内业务实现拨
备前利润508.83亿元,比上年同期增加127.38亿元,增幅达34.1%
全年消化历史包袱994代 884.5亿元,比上年多消化583.5亿元.

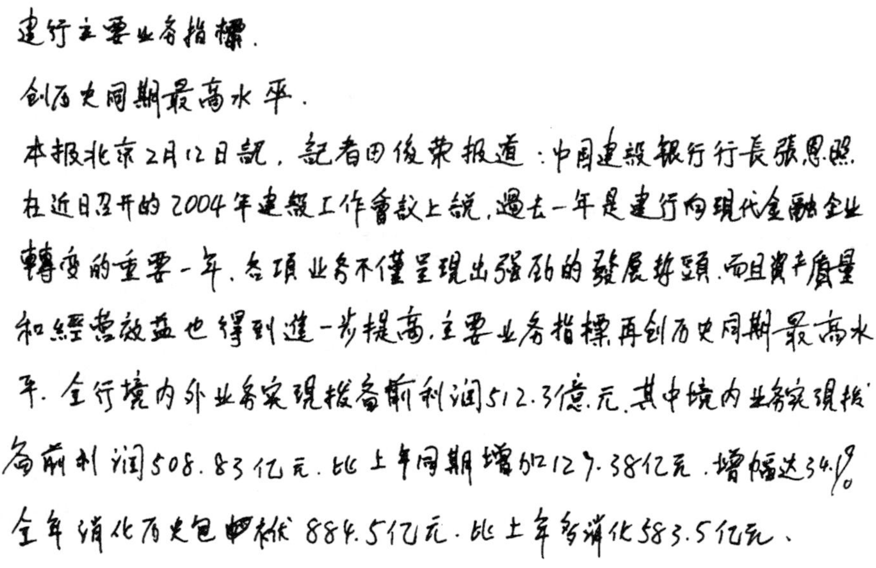

Fig. 2.15 A piece of handwriting with an erasure. Reprinted from Ref. Su et al. (2007a), with kind permission from Springer Science + Business Media

Second, analyzing the occurrences in each month, we can also infer that erasures are stable phenomena. On average, there are 38–39 occurrences per month with a concentrated derivation.

Third, the erasing marks show high possibility to be modeled by clustering them. There are 12 types of marks, however, the most commonly used ones mainly fall in four types and the sum of them makes 88 % of all.

In summary, erasing is a common and natural phenomenon stemming from real handwriting, and we should properly model them in order to acquire a sound

Table 2.6 Statistics on erasure

Mark	Jan.	Feb.	Mar.	Apr.	May	June	July	Aug.	Sep.	Oct.	Total
\	19	20	7	27	3	13	6	15	15	8	133
\\	12	12	9	11	5	3	11	21	10	11	105
•	4	7	12	7	10	5	10	3	1	4	63
\	8	5	3	6	1	6	–	–	2	3	34
≡	–	5	1	–	5	1	–	1	–	3	16
=	1	7	–	–	–	–	–	2	–	3	13
°	2	1	1	–	1	2	1	1	2	–	11
–	–	–	–	1	–	–	–	–	–	2	3
//	1	–	–	–	–	–	–	–	–	–	1
×	–	–	–	1	–	–	–	–	–	–	1
()	–	–	–	1	–	–	–	–	–	–	1
/	–	–	–	–	–	–	–	–	–	–	1
Total	47	57	33	54	25	30	28	43	30	35	382

Reprinted from Ref. Su et al. (2007a), with kind permission from Springer Science + Business Media

recognition performance. It is good news that the erasing marks manifest an excellent grouping possibility and that gives a promise for erasure modeling.

2.5.3 Miswriting Statistics

Miswriting in handwriting means what have been written are different from the appointed ones. It can be classified into three types: deletion, insertion, and substitution. Miswriting may hurt the linguistic context. However, it may not necessarily do that, and in some settings it even facilitates the context. For example, miswriting "建行工作" (in Chinese Pinyin: jian-hang-gong-zuo) as "建设工作" (in Chinese Pinyin: jian-she-gong-zuo) will improve the performance in trigram environment (see Eq. (2.4) to get a illustration).

$$
\begin{aligned}
& \frac{p(04年建设工作)}{p(04年建行工作)} \\
& \approx \frac{p(设|建年)\,p(工|设建)\,p(作|工设)}{p(行|建年)\,p(工|行建)\,p(作|工行)} \\
& \approx \frac{C(年建设)C(建设工)C(设工作)C(建行)C(行工)}{C(年建行)C(建行工)C(行工作)C(建设)C(设工)} \\
& = \frac{156\times1885\times635\times561\times1354}{6\times3\times1146\times109621\times1905} = 32.93 \gg 1
\end{aligned}
\tag{2.4}
$$

Table 2.7 Statistics of miswriting

(a) *Miswriting characters (unit: character)*			
Total	Deletion	Insertion	Substitution
2280	1884	110	274
(b) *Miswriting blocks and its linguistic effect (unit: block)*			
Total	Hurting context	Favoring context	
824	274	281	

Reprinted from Ref. Su et al. (2007a), with kind permission from Springer Science + Business Media

We calculate the miswriting occurrences excluding punctuation, since there present no punctuation in some applications, for example, automatic document image summarizing. At this stage, we integrate the decisions from three local language holders to determine whether the miswriting hurt the linguistic context or not. The term "context" here refers to two characters before and after the miswriting block. The result is summarized in Table 2.7. From Table 2.7a, we can see that the deleted characters are the most frequently occurred among the three classes. This fact leads us to infer: In handcopying activity, it is easier to miss characters than other miswriting cases. In Table 2.7b, there are 824 miswriting blocks totally, however, only 274 out of them hurt linguistic context.

Such imperfect situation has never happened yet in optical character recognition history, since all of the recognition algorithms are evaluated in ideal handwriting environment. Whether we should use SLM or not will not be as obvious as before. Suppose the recognition rate without SLM is 65 %, 80 % after SLM, and there is no rejection. It is interesting to see that the role of SLM is mainly determined by the degree of context hurting. If the recognition rate of hurting portion is larger than 35 %, SLM will be an essential stage; otherwise, there is no simple answer.

If we further analyze the substituted blocks, we may infer some tips concerning nerve mechanism of Chinese handcopying (Fu et al. 2002) which is out of the scope of this book.

2.6 Application of HIT-MW Database

Our database can support experiments in a more real aspect than character level database. At least but not limited to following four research directions can be emerged. Most of them are rarely or never explored yet.

(1) Real text line segmentation. Each piece of handwriting in our database is produced naturally by participant with no rules, resulting in a great number of real text lines. As expressed in Sect. 2.4.4, using global projection method directly, only 51.92 % of them can be correctly separated. The failure lies in irregular text lines. As soon as single text line is concerned, irregularity mainly

comes from skew line or undulate line. When considering adjacent text lines, there exist overlapping lines and touching ones. So, HIT-MW can be used to develop fine text line segmentation algorithms.

(2) Real and general handwriting recognition. Our database is produced with linguistic context and it is sampled from natural handwriting. Besides hand-printed characters, slant and cursive ones are of great quantity. In addition, erasures are presented. As manifested in Sect. 2.5.2, without modeling them, the recognition rate will suffer a bit. In this complex environment, more advanced techniques are needed.

(3) SLM in real situation. As we know, SLM is essential for general domain recognition. However, in our database, whether we should use SLM or not is not as clear as before due to them is writing and outlier (such as erasures). In addition, how to efficiently incorporate the SLM into the handwritten text recognition framework raises a new problem.

(4) Segmentation-free recognition. Current Chinese character recognition algorithms are all segmentation-based. As mentioned in Sect. 2.1, character recognition is a prone-to-error step. Unlikely, segmentation-free recognition deals with segmentation and recognition together and good optimal results may be gained easily. There are good reasons to explore the Chinese handwriting recognition from segmentation-free strategy. HIT-MW database provides such possibility.

2.7 Discussions and Conclusions

HIT-MW database inherits data sparseness from natural language, since texts are sampled from corpus. Character frequency of database is shown in Table 2.8. We can see that only a small portion of characters occur frequently. For example, only 1,853 ones out of 3,041 characters occur more than five times. This phenomenon can save our time and resource by pouring most efforts on most frequently used characters. However, as soon as the seldom-occurred characters concerned, there are too small number of samples for training. To overcome the data sparseness of

Occurrences	# of Characters
≥ 1000	16
≥ 100	456
≥ 10	1469
≥ 5	1853

Table 2.8 Character frequency of HIT-MW database

Reprinted from Ref. Su et al. (2007a), with kind permission from Springer Science + Business Media

our database and obtain complete flGBset, we can incorporate character level databases (such as IAAS-4M, HCL2000) into our database.

The handwritten Chinese text database discussed in this chapter addresses several important aspects not covered by most other databases. It is naturally written by multiple writers. Hence, there are real text lines and real handwriting phenomena. In addition, not only texts are well sampled, but also writers are carefully determined, resulting in a sound sampling of Chinese handwriting.

The original purpose of HIT-MW database is to facilitate the fundamental study on Chinese handwriting recognition from a brand new perspective. Many new research directions can be emerged, such as real text line segmentation, real and general handwriting recognition, SLM in real situation, segmentation-free recognition. Study on them may promote the real-world Chinese handwriting recognition greatly.

The database can be downloaded freely. The latest details are available at https://sites.google.com/site/hitmwdb/. In addition, the ground truth and the grayscale version of the database are also available upon request (Please contact hitmwdb@gmail.com).

References

U. Bhattacharya, B.B. Chaudhuri, Databases for research on recognition of handwritten characters of Indian scripts, in *Proceedings of the 8th International Conference on Document Analysis and Recognition*, Seoul, pp. 789–793 (2005)

R.G. Casey, E. Lecolinet, A survey of methods and strategies in character segmentation. IEEE Trans. Pattern Anal. Mach. Intell. **18**(7), 690–706 (1996)

Q. Fu, X. Ding, C. Liu, A new AdaBoost algorithm for large scale classification and its application to Chinese handwritten character recognition, in *ICFHR*, pp. 43–48 (2008)

S. Fu, Y. Chen, S. Smith, S. Iversen, P.M. Matthews, Effects of word form on brain processing of written Chinese. NeuroImage **17**(3), 1538–1548 (2002)

Y. Ge, Q. Huo, Z.D. Feng, Offline recognition of handwritten Chinese characters using Gabor features, CDHMM modeling and MCE training, in *Proceedings of the IEEE International Conference on Acoustics, Speech and Signal Processing*, Orlando, pp. 1053–1056 (2002)

General Administration of Technology of the People's Republic of China, *Code of Chinese Graphic Character Set for Information Interchange–Primary Set* (Standard Press of China, Beijing, 1980). (in Chinese)

D. Guillevic, C.Y. Suen, Recognition of legal amounts on bank cheques. Pattern Anal. Appl. **1**(1), 28–41 (1998)

I. Guyon, L. Schomaker, R. Plamondon, M. Liberman, S. Janet, UNIPEN project of on-line data exchange and recognizer benchmarks, in *Proceedings of 12th ICPR*, pp. 29–33 (1994)

W. Highleyman, An analog method for character recognition. IRE Trans. Electron. Comput. **EC-10**, 502–512 (1961)

J. Hull, A database for handwritten text recognition research. IEEE Trans. Pattern Anal. Mach. Intell. **16**(5), 550–554 (1994)

L. Jin, Study on handprinted Chinese character recognition. Ph.D. thesis, South China University of Technology, Guangzhou, 1996 (in Chinese)

L. Jin, Y. Gao, G. Liu, Y. Li, K. Ding, SCUT-COUCH2009—a comprehensive online unconstrained Chinese handwriting database and benchmark evaluation. Int. J. Doc. Anal. Recogn. **14**(1), 53–64 (2011)

E. Kavallieratou, N. Liolios, E. Koutsogeorgos, N. Fakotakis, G. Kokkinakis, The GRUHD database of Greek unconstrained handwriting, in *Proceedings of the 6th International Conference on Document Analysis and Recognition*, Seattle, pp. 561–565 (2001)

D.H. Kim, Y.S. Hwang, S.T. Park, E.J. Kim, S.H. Paek, S.Y. Bang, Handwritten Korean character image database PE92. IEICE Trans. Inf. Syst. **E79-D**(7), 943–950 (1996)

G. Kim, V. Govindaraju, S.N. Srihari, An architecture for handwritten text recognition systems. Int. J. Doc. Anal. Recogn. **2**(1), 37–44 (1999)

H.I. Koo, N.I. Cho, Text-line extraction in handwritten Chinese documents based on an energy minimization framework. IEEE Trans. Image Process. **21**(3), 1169–1175 (2012)

Z. Liang, P. Shi, A metasynthetic approach for segmenting handwritten Chinese character strings. Pattern Recogn. Lett. **26**(10), 1498–1511 (2005)

C.-L. Liu, M. Koga, H. Fujisawa, Lexicon-driven segmentation and recognition of handwritten character strings for Japanese address reading. IEEE Trans. Pattern Anal. Mach. Intell. **24**(11), 1425–1437 (2002)

C.-L. Liu, F. Yin, D.-H. Wang, Q.-F. Wang, CASIA online and offline Chinese handwriting databases. in ICDAR pp. 37–41 (2011)

Y.J. Liu, J.W. Tai, J. Liu, An introduction to the 4 million handwriting Chinese character samples library, in: *Proceedings of the International Conference on Chinese Computing and Orient Language Processing*, Changsha, pp. 94–97 (1989)

U. Marti, H. Bunke, The IAM-database: an English sentence database for off-line handwriting recognition. Int. J. Doc. Anal. Recogn. **5**(1), 39–46 (2002)

U.V. Marti, H. Bunke, A full English sentence database for off-line handwriting recognition, in *Proceedings of the 5th International Conference on Document Analysis and Recognition*, Bangalore, pp. 705–708 (1999)

Ministry of Education, *Educational Statistics Yearbook of 1998* (People's Education Press, Beijing, 1998). (in Chinese)

S. Mori, K. Yamamoto, H. Yamada, T. Saito, On a handprinted Kyoiku-Kanji character data base. Bull. Electrotech. Lab. **43**(11–12), 752–773 (1979)

J.H. Munson, Experiments in the recognition of hand-printed text, part 1-character recognition, in *Proceedings of the Fall Joint Computer Conference*, San Francisco, pp. 1125–1125 (1968)

M. Nakagawa, T. Higashiyama, Y. Yamanaka, S. Sawada, L. Higashigawa, K. Akiyama, On-line handwritten character pattern database sampled in a sequence of sentences without any writing instructions, in *Proceedings of the Fourth International Conference on Document Analysis and Recognition*, Ulm, pp. 376–381 (1997)

National Bureau of Statistics of China, *China Statistical Year-book 2004* (China Statistics Press, Beijing, 2005) (in Chinese)

N. Otsu, A threshold selection method from gray-level histogram. IEEE Trans. Syst. Man Cybern. **SMC-9**(1), 62–66 (1979)

J.S. Park, H.J. Kang, S.W. Lee, Automatic quality measurement of gray-scale handwriting based on extended average entropy. in Proceedings of the 15th international conference on pattern recognition, Barcelona (2000)

T. Saito, H. Yamada, K. Yamamoto, On the data base ETL9 of handprinted characters in JIS Chinese characters and its analysis. IEICE Trans. **J68-D**(4), 757–764 (1985)

K. Sayre, Machine recognition of handwritten words: a project report. Pattern Recogn. **5**(3), 213–228 (1973)

A.W. Senior, A.J. Robinson, An off-line cursive handwriting recognition system. IEEE Trans. Pattern Anal. Mach. Intell. **20**(3), 309–321 (1998)

T.-H. Su, T.-W. Zhang, D.-J. Guan, Corpus-based HIT-MW database for offline recognition of general-purpose Chinese handwritten text. Int. J. Doc. Anal. Recogn. **10**(1), 27–38 (2007a)

T.-H. Su, T.-W. Zhang, H.-J. Huang, Y. Zhou, Skew detection for Chinese handwriting by horizontal stroke histogram, in *IEEE Proceedings of the 9th International Conference on Document Analysis and Recognition*, pp. 899–903 (2007b)

T. Su, T. Zhang, H. Huang, G. Xue, Z. Zhao, Transformation-based hierarchical decision rules using genetic algorithms and its application to handwriting recognition domain, in *IEEE Congress on Evolutionary Computation*, pp. 951–956 (2008)

C.Y. Suen, M. Berthod, S. Mori, Automatic recognition of handprinted characters—the state of the art. Proc. IEEE **68**(4), 469–487 (1980)

C.Y. Suen, C. Nadal, R. Legault, T.A. Mai, L. Lam, Computer recognition of unconstrained handwritten numerals. Proc. IEEE **80**(7), 1162–1180 (1992)

L.-T. Tu, Y.S. Lin, C.P. Yeh, I.S. Shyu, J.L. Wang, K.H. Joe, W.W. Lin, Recognition of handprinted Chinese characters by feature matching, in *Proceedings of the 1st National Workshop on Character Recognition*, pp. 166–175 (1991)

C. Viard-Gaudin, P.M. Lallican, S. Knerr, P. Binter, The IRESTE On/Off (IRONOFF) dual handwriting database, in *Proceedings of the 5th International Conference on Document Analysis and Recognition*, Bangalore, pp. 455–458 (1999)

A. Vinciarelli, S. Bengio, H. Bunke, Offline recognition of unconstrained handwritten texts using HMMs and statistical language models. IEEE Trans. Pattern Anal. Mach. Intell. **26**(6), 709–720 (2004)

Y. Wu, X. Ding, *Character Recongition: Theory, Method and Implementation* (Higher Education Press, Beijing, 1992) (in Chinese)

M.E. Yacoubi, M. Gilloux, J.M. Bertille, A statistical approach for phrase location and recognition within a text line: an application to street name recognition. IEEE Trans. Pattern Anal. Mach. Intell. **24**(2), 172–188 (2002)

F. Yin, C.-L. Liu, Handwritten Chinese text line segmentation by clustering with distance metric learning. Pattern Recogn. **42**(12), 3146–3157 (2009)

F. Yin, C.-L. Liu, A variational Bayes method for handwritten text line segmentation, in *ICDAR*, pp. 436–440 (2009b)

F. Yin, Q.-F. Wang, C.-L. Liu, A tool for ground-truthing text lines and characters in off-line handwritten Chinese documents, in *ICDAR*, pp. 951–955 (2009)

H. Zhang, J. Guo, Introduction to HCL2000 database, in *Proceedings of Sino-Japan Symposium on Intelligent Information Networks*, Beijing (2000)

S. Zhou, Q. Chen, X. Wang, HIT-OR3C: an opening recognition corpus for Chinese characters, in *Proceedings of the 9th IAPR International Workshop on Document Analysis Systems* (2010)

M. Zimmermann, H. Bunke, N-gram language models for offline handwritten text recognition, in *9th International Workshop on Frontiers in Handwriting Recognition*, Kokubunji, pp. 203–208 (2004)

Chapter 3
Integrated Segmentation-Recognition Strategy

Abstract Reliable recognition of realistic Chinese handwriting is of overwhelming interest yet remains a challenging undertaking. Both sufficient training samples and advanced learning methods are critical to identifying the underlying symbols of a string image. This chapter first outlines two integrated segmentation-recognition reference systems. Then five sophisticated techniques are explored to improve the recognition accuracy or reduce the training costs. Among them, two techniques, PL-MQDF and active set, deal with isolated character classification; others are used to address natural handwriting recognition. String-level training is applied to Chinese handwriting recognition in order to provide robust training. To expand the training data, a perturbation model has been utilized for synthesizing string samples; linguistic constraints are also incorporated. Experiments are conducted to verify the techniques and steady improvements are demonstrated.

3.1 Introduction

Integrated segmentation-recognition strategy is initially introduced in digit string recognition (Fujisawa et al. 1992). The string sample is over-segmented into components and multiple hypotheses are generated. These hypotheses are represented in terms of a network of grouped components. A character classifier is used to score the grouped components. The path with the highest recognition scoring is selected. Recently, the strategy is applied to Chinese handwriting recognition.

This chapter addresses the realistic Chinese handwriting recognition problem using integrated segmentation-recognition strategy. The reference systems are given first in Sect. 3.2. Sophisticated algorithms are utilized to improve the recognition accuracy or reduce the training cost in the Sects. 3.3, 3.4, 3.5, 3.6, and 3.7. Finally, the efficacy of these algorithms is evaluated in Sect. 3.8.

T. Su, *Chinese Handwriting Recognition: An Algorithmic Perspective*,   49
SpringerBriefs in Electrical and Computer Engineering,
DOI: 10.1007/978-3-642-31812-2_3, © The Author(s) 2013

3.2 Reference Systems

Two kinds of reference systems are described. One is segmentation-based system whose simplification serves a good starting point. The other is integrated segmentation-recognition baseline system.

3.2.1 Segmentation-Based Baseline Systems

For segmentation-based system, character segmentation process attempts to separate each character first, then the isolated handwritten Chinese character recognition is triggered to identify the character segment, as illustrated in Fig. 3.1. Two character segmentation approaches, Hong algorithm (Hong et al. 1998) and Liu algorithm (Liu et al. 2002), will be provided in Sect. 3.2.1.2. First of all, we briefly describe the process to design an isolated Chinese character recognizer.

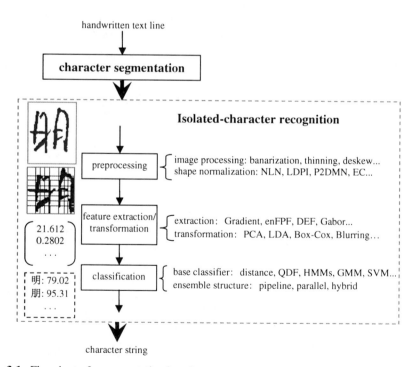

Fig. 3.1 Flowchart of a segmentation-based system

3.2.1.1 Isolated Chinese Character Recognizer

Great advances have been achieved during the last three decades, covering shape normalization, feature extraction, classifier design etc. Nonlinear normalization (Tsukumo and Tanaka 1988), directional feature (e.g. Gradient feature (Liu 2007)) with blurring (Iijima et al. 1972), and modified quadratic discriminant function (MQDF) (Kimura et al. 1987) are the three most significant fruits (Fujisawa 2008).

To develop a baseline system, nonlinear shape normalization, directional feature extraction, and MQDF classifier will be employed. To reduce the within-class dispersions of character shape, nonlinear normalization developed by (Tsukumo and Tanaka 1988) is applied. To determine the aspect ratio, sine aspect ratio is selected $(R_2 = [\sin(\pi R_1/2)]^{0.5}$, cf. Ref. (Cheriet et al. 2007) for more technical detail).

Then the directional features are extracted. The process for four plane feature and its enhanced version can be found in Chaps. 4, 5. Thus, we just present the extraction process for gradient features (Cheriet et al. 2007). The gradient can be computed on the normalized image using the Sobel operator, which has two masks in x and y axes. To obtain directional histogram features, the gradient vector is decomposed into components in eight standard directions. The length of each component is assigned to the corresponding direction plane at the pixel (x, y). The directional planes are formed by decomposing the gradient vectors at all pixels. In addition, we merge each pair of directional planes of opposite directions into orientation plane. Also a blurring process (the planes are smoothed with a Gaussian filter ($\sigma_x = 3.6$, filter size of 11 by 11)) is performed for reducing noise. As a result, four gradient planes are generated. To each character sample, a 256-dimensional feature vector is formed.

In Bayesian classification, we get the quadratic discriminant function (QDF) under the assumptions of multivariate Gaussian density and equal a priori probabilities

$$d_Q^2(x, \omega_i) = (x - \mu_i)^\mathrm{T}\Sigma_i^{-1}(x - \mu_i) + \ln|\Sigma_i|, \qquad (3.1)$$

where μ_i and Σ_i are the mean vector and covariance matrix of class ω_i, respectively. The modified QDF (MQDF) further replaces the minor eigenvalues with a larger constant (Kimura et al. 1987):

$$g_2(x, \omega_i) = \sum_{j=1}^{k} \lambda_{ij}^{-1}\left[\phi_{ij}^{T}(x - \mu_i)\right]^2 + \sum_{j=1}^{k} \log \lambda_{ij} \\ + \delta_i^{-1}r_i(x) + (d - k)\log \delta_i \qquad (3.2)$$

where λ_{ij} is the jth largest eigenvalue of Σ_i, ϕ_{ij} is the corresponding eigenvector, δ_i is the truncated minor eigenvalues, k denotes the number of principal axes, and $r_i(x)$ is the residual of subspace projection:

$$r_i(x) = \|x - \mu_i\|^2 - \sum_{j=1}^{k} \left[(x - \mu_i)^T \phi_{ij} \right]^2. \tag{3.3}$$

MQDF falls into generative model and its parameter set $\Theta_i = \{\lambda_{ij}, \delta_i, \mu_i, \phi_{ij}\}$ is commonly derived from the estimation of maximum likelihood.

Minor modification can also be applied, considering the unbalanced distributions of different classes:

$$
\begin{aligned}
g_3(x, \omega_i) = & \sum_{j=1}^{k} \frac{1}{\lambda_{ij}} \left[\phi_{ij}^T (x - \mu_i) \right]^2 + \sum_{j=k+1}^{d} \frac{1}{\delta_i} \left[\phi_{ij}^T (x - \mu_i) \right]^2 \\
& + \sum_{j=1}^{k} \log \lambda_{ij} + (d - k) \log \delta_i - 2 \log P(\omega_i)
\end{aligned} \tag{3.4}
$$

For our modification is applied to MQDF2, we denote above classifier as MQDF3 (Su et al. 2009). In addition, special attention is given to the character class of small sample size. If the number of samples is below 10, λ_{ij} and ϕ_{ij} will be degenerated as the eigenvalue and eigenvector of global covariance matrix. The character segment will be classified into class j, if

$$g_3(x, \omega_j) = \min_i g_3(x, \omega_i). \tag{3.5}$$

Other techniques are usually employed to increase its robustness. To make it more Gaussian-like, Box-Cox transformation (Heiden and Groen 1997) with the power of 0.5 is utilized. Linear discriminant analysis (LDA) (Duda et al. 2001) is helpful to a practical recognizer.

3.2.1.2 Character Segmentation Approaches

Hong algorithm is originally proposed in Ref. (Hong et al. 1998). However, to simplify the process, only the basic segmentation and the fine segmentation stages are used to generate the candidate paths.

In the basic segmentation stage, five space thresholds are selected to establish five versions of segmentation results. First, text line is projected onto x axis. The projection profile is then scanned from left to right, and the position is saved as boundary where the width of that space zone surpasses a certain threshold. This chapter sets the thresholds as 17, 13, 9, 5, and 1 pixel(s), respectively. The five results are ordered in their width variance, and two results with smallest variance are passed to the following stage.

Considering the characters with left–right structure and touching characters, a fine segmentation is conducted further. As the first step, small segments are merged. When the width of a segment is smaller than half the average character width, it should be merged into its neighbor segment. If the width variance of all segments decreases, current merging is accepted. Otherwise, current merging is discarded. Next, splitting is performed to each segment whose width is bigger than double of the average width. New boundary is searched within a region whose width is of one-fourth the average character width around the center of that segment. If current splitting decreases the width variance of all segments, it is valid. Otherwise, it is discarded.

Above process is stopped until all segments are inspected. And finally, the segmentation result with minimal variance is selected as the final segmentation path.

In Liu algorithm (Liu et al. 2002), a text line image is represented as a sequence of connected components (CCs), and each CC is represented as a set of black runs. The segmentation process composes of two steps: connected component analysis and touching pattern splitting.

In a text line, the CCs overlapping in writing direction likely come from the same character. To decide whether to merge two adjacent components, a normalized overlapping degree (*nmovlp*) between them is computed. If $nmovp > 0$, the two components are to be merged. After recursive merging, each component (not necessarily connected now) is referred to as an image segment. The segments of potential touching patterns are detected and undergo splitting. After splitting, if any segment is still judged to be a multiple pattern, it is split forcedly according to the projection profile. As a result, one or more consecutive segments are combined into candidate character patterns. This algorithm is developed for the character segmentation of Japanese address. In Ref. (Liu et al. 2002), no confidence information from Chinese character classifier is employed. An enhanced version of this algorithm is used in this book where a classifier is used to verify the character segmentation.

3.2.2 Integrated Segmentation-Recognition Baseline System

Integrated segmentation-recognition strategy aims to perform character segmentation and recognition in one step, utilizing multiple contexts. The flowchart of a baseline system within this strategy is showed in Fig. 3.2. It is constructed as follows. First, the input text line image is over-segmented into primitive segments using Liu algorithm, in hoping that the true character boundaries are included.

Second, the consecutive segments are combined to form candidate patterns and each candidate pattern is represented in a 160-dimensional feature vector of gradient direction, and is assigned a classification score by the MQDF classifier, which has 40 eigenvectors for each class, generating the segmentation-recognition lattice.

Last, each path is evaluated by the character classification confidence or even language score. The optimal path, including segmentation and recognition result, can be finally identified using the beam search technique.

The recognition task for Chinese text line can be expressed as a path searching problem, utilizing candidate character segmentation, character confidence, and

Fig. 3.2 Flowchart of an integrated segmentation-recognition baseline system

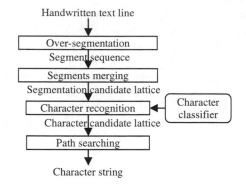

other information. In (Wang et al. 2009), the path evaluation function is expressed as a likelihood score based on Bayesian framework:

$$f(\mathbf{O}, S) = \lambda_1 \log P(S) + \lambda_i \Sigma_i k_i \log P(\mathbf{o}_i | s_i). \tag{3.6}$$

The path of top score over all combinations ((**O**, *S*) gives the segmentation and recognition result.

3.3 Perceptron Learning of MQDF

MQDF, originally proposed by Kimura (Kimura et al. 1987), is a compact Gaussian classifier with the state-of-the-art performance in handwritten character recognition. MQDF reparameterizes the covariance matrix into eigenvalues and eigenvectors and truncates the small eigenvalues to denoise the unstable estimation. MQDF often generalizes better than regular quadratic discriminant function (QDF) and it runs faster and requires lower storage by product. Traditionally, the parameters of MQDF are derived from maximum likelihood estimator (MLE) which is a generative method, thus the learning process is not directly related to its classification performance.

Previously, minimum classification error (MCE) criterion is tried on MQDF (Liu et al. 2004; Wang and Huo 2010; Liu and Ding 2005). The MCE criterion is well-known in speech recognition (Juang et al. 1997) and it is used to adjust parameters of MQDF (MCE-MQDF). (Liu et al. 2004) conduct thorough investigation on MCE-MQDF and the experiments on digit recognition justify its superior. Due to the intensive computation burden, MCE-MQDF is applied on Chinese handwritten character recognition where just the mean vectors and eigenvalues of MQDF are adjusted (Liu and Ding 2005). Recently, MCE-MQDF with a revised loss function is applied on Chinese handwritten character recognition with the help of parallelization programming and they only update the mean vectors (Wang and Huo 2010).

Despite rapid advances in computer speed, heavy training burden is still one of the biggest problems for such discriminative learning methods.

To overcome the shortcomings of MCE-MQDF, we propose a new method for discriminative learning of MQDF in the context of large-category learning task. Our model is based on one of the oldest Perceptron algorithm (Rosenblatt 1958) that is, we pursue for Perceptron learning of modified quadratic discriminant function (PL-MQDF). It is worthy to further highlight our model from machine learning perspective. PL-MQDF is a quadratic Perceptron, which is different from the traditional nonlinear extension of linear models. Mostly, linear models are extended into their nonlinear counterpart via kernel trick or explicit mapping. When the dataset is large, kernel methods will produce many support vectors which is time-consuming in evaluation. Explicit quadratic mapping requires a large memory to save the mapped features, and it can only learn a regular QDF. The MQDF cannot be equipped with these two tricks for its complex nonlinear structure. Therefore, PL-MQDF is irreplaceable by those two nonlinear extensions. What is more, PL-MQDF scales well to large-scale applications.

However, the direct use of Perceptron suffers from overfitting and slow training. Two endeavors are done to make Perceptron generalize better and scale better. First of all, we regularize the objective function through a dynamic margin constraint to achieve a better generalization performance. On the other hand, active set technique is equipped with Perceptron; most computation costs are saved, meanwhile without much loss in accuracy. This subsection provides the details of regularization; the active set technique is described in Sect. 3.4.

3.3.1 Perceptron Learning

Hybrid generative and discriminative models will give higher classification accuracy, as well as the resistance to outliers (Liu et al. 2004). Perceptron is used for discriminative learning of MQDF. First, the misclassification measure on a pattern from class ω_c is defined, following (Juang et al. 1997):

$$h(x, \Theta_c, \Theta_r) = d^2(x, \omega_c) - d^2(x, \omega_r), \qquad (3.7)$$

where $d^2(x, \omega_r)$ is the score of the closest rival class $d^2(x, \omega_r) = \min_{i \in M} d^2(x, \omega_r)$ with M is the candidate set exluding c. The meaning of $d^2(x, \omega_r)$ and $d^2(x, \omega_r)$ is illustrated in Fig. 3.3. Using Perceptron learning, the goal is to minimize

$$L_p = \sum_{x_n \in E} d^2(x_n, \omega_c) - d^2(x_n, \omega_r), \qquad (3.8)$$

where $E = \{x | h(x, \Theta_c, \Theta_r) > 0\}$.

On instance x_n, stochastic gradient descent (SGD) updates as

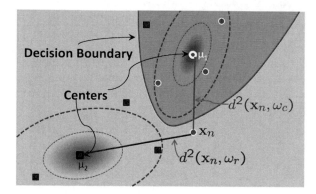

Fig. 3.3 Illustration of $d^2(x, \omega_r)$ and $d^2(x, \omega_c)$. Sample x_n belongs to the class represented by *circled* points

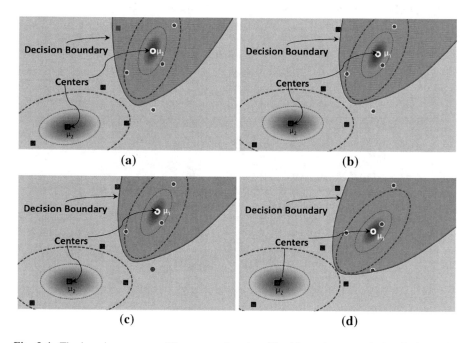

Fig. 3.4 The learning process of Perceptron learning. The *blue* points are misclassified samples as showed in (**a**) and (**c**), and (**b**) and (**d**) adjust the parameters as needed, **a** step 1: locate an error, **b** step 1: update the parameters, **c** step 2: locate an error, **d** step 2: update the parameters

$$\Theta_i \leftarrow \Theta_i - \eta \frac{\partial\{d^2(x_n, \omega_c) - d^2(x_n, \omega_r)\}}{\partial\Theta_i}, \tag{3.9}$$

where η is the learning step. The learning process is depicted in Fig. 3.4.

3.3.2 Dynamic Margin Regularization

The direct use of Perceptron suffers from overfitting and slow training. This section provides the essential building blocks for an effective and efficient PL-MQDF.

Margin constraint is imposed to ensure a good generalization. If the difference between the squared distance from x to ω_r and that from x to ω_c does not exceed a margin, a margin error is triggered. That is, not only the misclassified samples, but also the correctly classified ones that near the decision boundary are used to update the parameters.

Analogous to (Cheng et al. 2009), the objective function with constant margin strength can be formulated as

$$L_p = \sum_{x_n \in E} d^2(x_n, \omega_c) - d^2(x_n, \omega_r) + \rho, \qquad (3.10)$$

where ρ is the margin strength and $\mathbf{E} = \{x|\ d^2(x, \omega_c) - d^2(x, \omega_r) > -\rho\}$.

Considering the large divergence of different classes, fixed margin may lose its precision. On every instance x, we seek a local margin proportional to the squared distance from x to ω_c. Then we would like to let all instances satisfy: $d^2(x, \omega_r) - d^2(x, \omega_c) > \rho d^2(x, \omega_c)$. Intuitively, x should be not only correctly classified but also kept away from the decision boundary, as illustrated in Fig. 3.5. We renew the misclassification measure

$$h(x, \Theta_c, \Theta_r) = (1 + \rho)d^2(x, \omega_c) - d^2(x, \omega_r), \qquad (3.11)$$

or

$$h(x, \Theta_c, \Theta_r) = \rho d^2(x, \omega_c) + \left[d^2(x, \omega_c) - d^2(x, \omega_r)\right]. \qquad (3.12)$$

We first consider Eq. (3.11). The first term penalizes large distances from x to its true class. The gradient of this term generates a pulling force that attracts the true class. The second term penalizes small distances from x to its most confusable class. The gradient of this term generates a pushing force that repels the rival class.

Fig. 3.5 Margin constraint is imposed to ensure a good generalization. The *red* sample in *top* middle violates margin constraint, though correctly classified

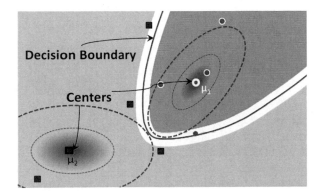

Moreover, the strength of pulling is larger than that of pushing and is determined by the intensity of ρ. We then consider Eq. (3.12). The role of the first term is the same as the term in Eq. (3.11). The remaining terms penalize the classification error. Their gradient generates a pushing force to make the difference of those squared distances larger. As a result, the empirical errors may be greatly decreased under these two terms.

Plugging in the dynamic margin, the objective function becomes:

$$L_p' = \sum_{x \in E} (1+\rho)d^2(x_n, \omega_c) - d^2(x_n, \omega_r), \qquad (3.13)$$

where $\mathbf{E} = \{x| \, d^2(x, \omega_c) - d^2(x, \omega_r) > - \, \rho \, d^2(x, \omega_c)\}$. The elements in $\mathbf{E}$ incur a classification error or violate the margin error. Only in Eq. (3.13) can the margin constraint be viewed as regularization to MLE. If ρ is 0, the model degenerates as a Perceptron without margin. On the contrary, we attain maximum likelihood estimation when ρ approaching to ∞.

At the tth iteration, Θ_c and Θ_r are updated on the erroneous instance x_n as:

$$\begin{cases} \Theta_c(t+1) \leftarrow \Theta_c(t) - (1+\rho)\eta_t \nabla d^2(x_n, \omega_c)\big|_{\Theta_c(t)} \\ \Theta_r(t+1) \leftarrow \Theta_r(t) + \eta_t \nabla d^2(x_n, \omega_r)\big|_{\Theta_r(t)} \end{cases}. \qquad (3.14)$$

We should highlight that Eq. (3.10) does not affect the learning rate in Eq. (3.9), while Eq. (3.13) changes the learning rate of Θ_c from η_t to $(1 + \rho)\eta_t$. If we specify the initial learning rate and the last one before halting as $1/t_0$ and $1/(mt_0)$, respectively, then the learning rate at tth step is set as:

$$\eta_t = \frac{T \times S}{t_0 \times (T \times S + (m - 1) \times (t - 1))}, \qquad (3.15)$$

where T is the total number of training rounds, S is the sample size.

There are two distinctions than MCE learning. First, the loss function is different. Perceptron employs a hinge-style loss; MCE uses a sigmoid function to approximate the 0–1 loss. Second, they vary in the update rule. Perceptron just considers the information from misclassified instances, while MCE absorbs information from all instances. Although their distinctions, many implementation tricks of MCE can be seamlessly adopted to Perceptron such as parameter transformation, partial derivation of squared distance (Cf. (Liu et al. 2004) for more details).

3.3.3   Interpretation

Our model is applicable to both MQDF and QDF. We show that the learning model of this section is a general framework covering learning vector quantization (LVQ) family. If we impose structural constraints on Σ_i, we obtain LVQ and its variants such as LVQ with class-independent weighting and LVQ with class-dependent weighting (Cf. (Jin et al. 2010)).

Case 1: Assuming $\forall i$, $\Sigma_i = \mathbf{I}$ ($\mathbf{I}$ is the identity matrix), Eq. (3.7) becomes:

$$
\begin{aligned}
h(x, \Theta_c, \Theta_r) &= \|x - \mu_c\|_2^2 - \|x - \mu_r\|_2^2 \\
&= -2\big(\|x - \mu_c\|_2 - \|x - \mu_r\|_2\big) \cdot \big(\|x - \mu_c\|_2 + \|x - \mu_r\|_2\big)
\end{aligned} \qquad (3.16)
$$

Using SGD w.r.t. μ_i, we get the LVQ classifier. The regularization of dynamic margin in Eq. (3.13) is similar to (Jin et al. 2010) and helps to enlarge the hypothesis margin. As shown in Crammer et al. (2002), maximizing hypothesis margin provides an upper bound of generalization error for LVQ.

Case 2: Assuming $\forall i$, $\Sigma_i = \mathrm{diag}\{w^1, \ldots, w^d\}$, Eq. (3.7) becomes:

$$
h(x, \Theta_c, \Theta_r) = \sum_{p=1}^{d} w^p \big(x^p - \mu_c^p\big)^2 - \sum_{p=1}^{d} w^p \big(x^p - \mu_r^p\big)^2, \qquad (3.17)
$$

and we get the LVQ with class-independent weighting. Even we can assume $\Sigma_i = \Sigma$ and fix it. We will run LVQ in a linear transformed space and all theoretical reasoning are still held.

Case 3: Assuming $\Sigma_i = \mathrm{diag}\{w_i^1, \ldots, w_i^d\}$ and omitting logarithmic terms, Eq. (3.7) becomes:

$$
h(x, \Theta_c, \Theta_r) = \sum_{p=1}^{d} w_c^p \big(x^p - \mu_c^p\big)^2 - \sum_{p=1}^{d} w_r^p \big(x^p - \mu_r^p\big)^2, \qquad (3.18)
$$

and we get the LVQ with class-dependent weighting. If we further relax the structural constraints to just require $\Sigma_i \geq 0$, we arrive at the learning model in this section.

3.4 Active Set Technique

We employ active set technique to speed up the training process of Perceptron algorithm. If an instance invokes a classification error or margin error, we say it "active". During the cycling once through the available training instances, all active instances form an active set for the subsequent rounds. Such procedure can be nested and active sets of different levels can be generated.

For demonstration purpose, we present two nested active sets similar to (Panagiotakopoulos and Tsampouka 2010). The first active set named AS_1 is composed of the instances from the full training dataset violating margin constraints. The second one named AS_2 is built from the active instances in AS_1. AS_2 is presented repetitively to the algorithm for N_2 passes. Then AS_1 comes back which is cycled once again to the algorithm. Each time AS_1 is under consideration, AS_2 is restarted. After N_1 times invoking of AS_1, we will resume to the full training dataset and the procedure starts all over again. The switching of above three sets is depicted in Fig. 3.6. The full training dataset is denoted as AS_0.

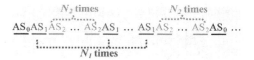

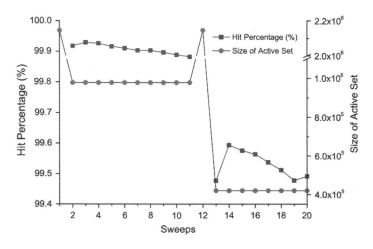

Fig. 3.6 The switching order of active sets. © [2011] IEEE. Reprinted, with permission, from Ref. (Su et al. 2011)

Fig. 3.7 The hit percentage versus the size of active set. © [2011] IEEE. Reprinted, with permission, from Ref. (Su et al. 2011)

We give a concrete example to show that the active set technique will not excessively drop the samples that should be used for learning in our setting. We select the Chinese handwritten character database as full training dataset and set $\{N_1 = 10, N_2 = 0\}$. During the first cycling through AS_0, we generate a AS_1. On each of the following 10 rounds, we first record all samples with margin error from AS_0 and the percentage of samples that can be found in AS_1 is called hit percentage. When the allowed rounds are exhausted, we generate a new AS_1 and restart the collection of hit percentage. After cycling 20 times, we stop it. The hit percentages of the process are shown in Fig. 3.7. We can see a high hit percentage and a large reduction in the size of active set.

3.5 String Sample Synthesizing

As more data win, synthesizing samples have attracted intensive study. Several methods for human-like writing generation are available. Guerfali and Plamondon (Guerfali and Plamondon 1995) propose a delta-log normal model which has been utilized to generate curvilinear strokes. Kokula (1994) describes script font ligature generation on-the-fly by optimizing a parametric curve between neighbor

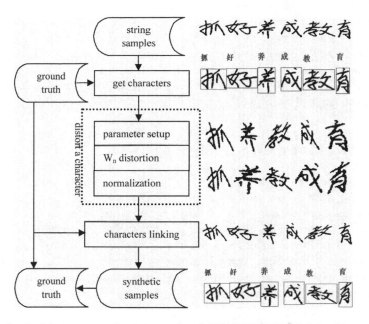

Fig. 3.8 Synthesizing process of string samples. © [2010] IEEE. Reprinted, with permission, from Ref. (Chen et al. 2010)

characters. Varga et al. (2006) perform a perturbation model for generating synthetic English text lines from naturally written text lines. Mori et al. (2000) develop a character generation method based on point correspondence between patterns. To our best of knowledge, the synthetic data used successfully to train recognizers are mainly related to the field of western character recognition and isolated Chinese handwritten character recognition (e.g. (Leung and Leung 2009)). Hence, we distort naturally written string samples to expand the training data and meet the requirements of string-level training.

Considering the heavy shortage of string samples in string-level training, expanding training set may improve the string recognition rates. Baird (2000) has pointed out that the size and quality of the training data have a major impact on the recognition performance. In Leung and Leung (2009), a perturbation model has been used to generate Chinese handwritten character samples by distorting the naturally written characters. In this section, we also apply it to generate Chinese handwritten string samples. Figure 3.8 shows the flowchart of synthesizing process.

3.5.1 String Sample Distortion

To get the information of each character, such as character boundary and character bitmap data, the system first read the ground truth file of the original string image. Then each character is distorted by the method in (Leung and Leung 2009) and normalized to the original size in string image. Finally, all the distorted characters are connected according to the original gap between characters. In the following, we demonstrate the distortion process of a character in string samples.

Denote the original character sample and synthetic one by $f(x, y)$ and $g(u,v)$, respectively. The distortion can be achieved via the mapping function h_x and h_y for all pixels in original character

$$\begin{cases} u = h_x(x,y) = w_n(a_1, b_1(x)) + k_1 y + c_1 \\ v = h_y(x,y) = w_n(a_2, b_2(y)) + k_2 x + c_2 \end{cases}, \tag{3.19}$$

where k_1 and k_2 are the shearing slopes randomly picked from $[-0.17, 0.17]$ and $[-0.2, 0.2]$, $a_1 \neq 0$ and $a_2 \neq 0$ are constants controlling the extent of local resizing (randomly taken from $[-1.6, 1.6]$), c_1 and c_2 are set x and y, respectively, $b_1(x)$ and $b_2(y)$ are functions to linearly scale the original coordinates to the interval $[0,1]$, and w_n is a nonlinear warping function for producing local variations on the size of subpatterns, which is randomly choosed as w_1 and w_2 with the probabilities of 0.8 and 0.2, respectively. Note that the parameters of w_n distortion are defined as (Leung and Leung 2009):

$$\begin{aligned} w_1 &= (1 - e^{-at})/(1 - e^{-a}) \\ w_2 &= \begin{cases} 0.5 w_1(a, 2t), & 0 \leq t \leq 0.5 \\ 0.5 + 0.5 w_1(-a, 2(t-0.5)), & 0.5 < t \leq 1 \end{cases} \end{aligned} \tag{3.20}$$

We can see that the mapping functions take care of both shearing and local resizing from Eqs. (3.19) and (3.20).

Figure 3.9 shows the natural string sample and synthesized string samples. Note that the figures are only for illustration purposes, and weaker distortions are actually used in our experiments.

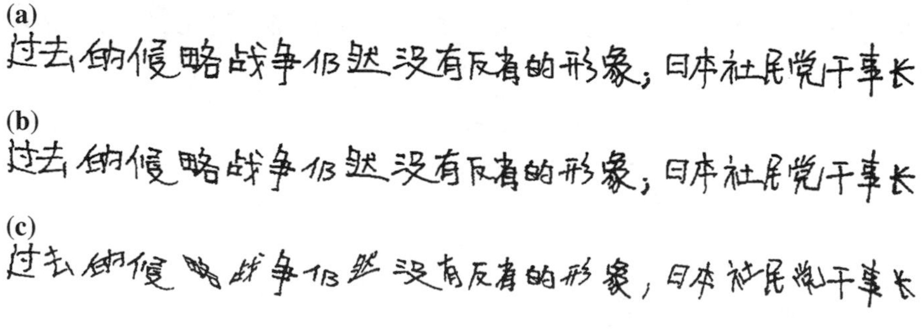

Fig. 3.9 Natural string samples and synthesized ones. © [2010] IEEE. Reprinted, with permission, from Ref. (Chen et al. 2010), **a** natural sample, **b** weak distortion, **c** strong distortion

3.5.2 *Verisimilitude Consideration*

There are two adversarial effects to enlarge the training set by synthetic samples. On the one hand, it increases the variability of the training set, which can be beneficial especially when the original training set is not large enough. On the other hand, it may generate characters and strings of rather unusual shapes, which may bias the recognizer toward unnatural handwritten styles. To reduce the latter effect, we should make sure that the synthetic samples look like the natural ones.

The verisimilitude of synthetic samples is mainly influenced by the distortion strength; in other words, the stronger the distortion, the lower verisimilitude the synthetic samples look like. In our implementation, two issues are considered. First, due to the random nature of distortion model and the complicated structure of Chinese character, some strokes inevitably break up or are even lost in the distortion process. We apply mean filter to smoothen the strokes and then binarize the image using a hard threshold (here the threshold is 4). Second, each distorted character is normalized to original character size in order to easily generate the ground truth file of each synthetic sample.

3.6 String-Level Training

String-level training has been tried for a decade. Subunit models are concatenated together to form a string and the underlying parameters are estimated in an embedding way. Good string recognition performance has been reported by string-level training in early works (Burges et al. 1992). Recently, appealing results for handwritten numeral string recognition (Liu and Katsumi 2004) have been achieved using MCE criteria, aiming to minimize the string recognition error (Juang et al. 1997). As mentioned previously, CDHMMs for sequential outputs are also based on embedding training. However, there is few practice of string-level training for Chinese handwriting recognition within the integrated segmentation-recognition approach, because databases including large string samples are available until recently.

In MCE-based string-level training, the string sample is matched with the genuine string class and the most rival class. The MCE criterion transforms the string recognition error, the contrast between the scores of genuine string class and competing string classes, into a probabilistic loss. The classifier parameters are updated by stochastic gradient descent with the aim of minimizing the probabilistic loss.

3.6.1 MCE Criterion

Let $\mathcal{D} = \{(X_n, y_n)|X_n \in \chi, y_n \in Y = \{1,...,C\}, n = 1 \sim N\}$ be training set. The goal of classification is to label an unknown sample X (string or character) based on discriminant score as: $j = \arg\max_i g_i(X, \Theta)$. Following Juang et al. (1997), the misclassification measure on a pattern from class c can be given:

$$h_c(X, \Theta) = -g_c(X, \Theta) + g_r(X, \Theta), \tag{3.21}$$

where $g_r(X, \Theta) = \max_{i \neq c} g_i(X, \Theta)$. The nondifferentiable 0–1 loss function is approximated

$$\ell_c(X_n, \Theta) = \ell_c(h_c) = \frac{1}{1 + e^{-\xi h_c}}, \tag{3.22}$$

where ξ is the scaling factor of sigmoid function.

On the training sample set, the empirical loss is

$$\begin{aligned} L_0 &= \frac{1}{N}\sum_{n=1}^{N}\sum_{i=1}^{C} \ell_i(X_n, \Theta)I(Y_n = i) \\ &= \frac{1}{N}\sum_{n=1}^{N} \ell_c(X_n, \Theta) \end{aligned}. \tag{3.23}$$

By stochastic gradient descent, the classifier parameters are updated on each input sample by

$$\Theta(t+1) = \Theta(t) - \varepsilon(t)\nabla\ell_c(X, \Theta)|_{\Theta=\Theta(t)}, \tag{3.24}$$

where $\varepsilon(t)$ is the learning step.

3.6.2 String-Level Training

A string image comprises a sequence of candidate patterns $X = x_1,..., x_P$ and the string class is denoted by a sequence of character classes $W = w_{i_1},..., w_{i_P}$. The discriminant score can be expressed as an average score

$$g(X, W, \Theta) = ND(X, W) = \frac{1}{P}\sum_{p=1}^{P} g(x_p, w_{i_p}). \tag{3.25}$$

where $g(x, w)$ measures the likelihood from x to w (e.g. MQDF).

Denote the genuine string by $W_c = w_{i1},..., w_{iP}$ and the closest competing string by $W_r = w_{j1},..., w_{jQ}$, corresponding to two sequences of segmented patterns $x_1^c,...,x_P^c$ and $x_1^r,...,x_Q^r$, respectively. The misclassification measure in Eq. (3.21) can be given

$$h_c(X, \Theta) = ND(X, W_r) - ND(X, W_c)$$

$$= \frac{1}{Q}\sum_{q=1}^{Q} g\left(x_q^r, w_{jq}\right) - \frac{1}{P}\sum_{p=1}^{P} g\left(x_p^c, w_{ip}\right). \tag{3.26}$$

Similarly, the classifier parameters are updated on training sample by stochastic gradient descent

$$\Theta(t+1) = \Theta(t) - \varepsilon(t)\nabla l_c(X, \Theta)|_{\Theta=\Theta(t)}$$
$$= \Theta(t) - \varepsilon(t)\xi l_c(1 - l_c)\nabla h_c(X, \Theta)|_{\Theta=\Theta(t)}, \tag{3.27}$$

where $\nabla h_c(X, \Theta)$ can be further derived as

$$\nabla h_c(X, \Theta) = \frac{1}{Q}\sum_{q=1}^{Q} \nabla g\left(x_q^r, w_{jq}\right) - \frac{1}{P}\sum_{p=1}^{P} \nabla g\left(x_p^c, w_{ip}\right). \tag{3.28}$$

Based on the fact that the partial derivative on a candidate pattern is independent of other nonoverlapping patterns, we perform the updating of Eq. (3.27) using the method in (Cheriet et al. 2007).

3.7 Linguistic Constraints

For natural language, characters or words do not occur arbitrarily in a text. Language models aim at capturing the constraints that are imposed on character sequences in a given language and they are widely used in speech recognition and handwriting recognition. The most frequently used language model is based on N-grams, which characterizes the statistical dependency between characters or words.

The prior probability of a sequence of characters $S = s_1,..., s_n$ can be described using a Markov chain

$$P(S) = p(s_1)p(s_2|s_1)...p(s_n|s_1, \ldots, s_{n-1}) = \prod_{i=1}^{n} p(s_i|s_1, \ldots, s_{i-1}), \tag{3.29}$$

In practice, the conditioning character history is usually truncated to $N-1$ characters to form N-gram model

$$P(S) = \prod_{i=1}^{n} p(s_i|s_{i-N+1}, \ldots, s_{i-1}), \tag{3.30}$$

where N is typically smaller than 5. This book merely uses 2-gram (bigram) for demonstration purpose:

$$P(S) = p(s_1) \prod_{i=2}^{n} p(s_i|s_{i-1}).$$

(3.31)

The bigram probabilities can be estimated from large text corpus by a maximum likelihood (ML) scheme

$$p(s_i|s_{i-1}) = \frac{C(s_{i-1}s_i)}{C(s_{i-1})},$$

(3.32)

where $C(.)$ means counting events. The major problem with this simple ML estimation scheme is data sparsity. Smoothing techniques (this book uses Katz smoothing (Katz 1987)) are used to mitigate.

3.8 Experiments

In Sect. 3.8.1, handwritten databases used in this chapter are introduced. Then algorithms are evaluated in the following subsections.

3.8.1 Databases

Both isolated handwritten character database and Chinese handwriting database are used to evaluate the recognition algorithms.

3.8.1.1 Isolated Handwritten Character Databases

Two handwritten digit databases, MNIST and USPS, are chosen to evaluate the PL-MQDF algorithm. MNIST database, the original 20 by 20 fine grayscale images are used to extract features (Liu et al. 2003). Three kinds of features are evaluated separately: *img*, *pca80*, *and e-grg* (Cf. (Liu et al. 2003) for more details). *img* is derived from arranging the image pixel into a 400D feature vector. *pca80* is processed by principal component analysis on *img* (from 400D to 80D). *e-grg* is 8-direction gradient features (200D). Likely, *img* and *e-grg* are extracted and evaluated on USPS database.

As for handwritten Chinese character database, CASIA-HWDB1.0 (DB1.0) and CASIA-HWDB1.1 (DB1.1) (Liu et al. 2011) are used to verify the efficacy of PL-MQDF. The samples of DB1.0 were written on forms with 4037 preprinted characters, and the samples of DB1.1 were written on forms with 3,926 preprinted characters. In either case, the character set contains 171 alphanumeric characters and symbols. The character set of DB1.0 also contains 3,866 Chinese characters,

3,740 of which are contained in GB2312-1980 level-1 set (GB1). The character set of DB1.1 contains exactly 3,755 Chinese characters of GB1. The Chinese characters of each set were preprinted in six different orders to balance the writing quality variation of each writer through the writing process.

Another handprinted Chinese character database called HCL2000 (Zhang and Guo 2000) is used to train character classifiers in Sects. 3.8.3.2, 3.8.2.3, and 3.8.3.4. It is released by Beijing University of Posts and Telecommunications, which contains 1,000 samples for each of the 3,755 characters.

3.8.1.2 HIT-MW Database

The benchmark data for handwriting recognition come from the HIT-MW database. We restrict the experimental dataset from 5,667 text lines. To partition the data into train, validation, and test sets, we consider the following procedure (the HIT-MW database and the experimental data in this book are available at: http://sites.google.com/site/hitmwdb).

(1) Randomly select 383 text lines as test set (8,471 characters).
(2) Within the 5,284 remainder text lines, discard the text lines which are written by the same writer of test set. By this way, only 3,172 text lines are retained for the following processing.
(3) Similar to step 1, draw 189 text lines uniformly out of 3,172 ones as validation set (4,100 characters).
(4) Further discard text lines written by the same writer of validation set (2,306 text lines are left).
(5) Among the 2,306 text lines, randomly select 953 ones as train set (20,701 characters).

This process is to reproduce a realistic scenario where the handwritten text lines for recognition in test set have not been seen before (in train or validation set). The validation set here is used to tune the parameters, such as the number of Gaussian components in mixture density and training iterations, which will be used to evaluate the recognizer's performance on test set. Some text lines selected from test set are demonstrated in Fig. 3.10.

3.8.2 Evaluation on Character Databases

Our investigation includes the error reduction and training time of PL-MQDF. Evaluation is conducted on both small-category learning task and large-category learning task. All the experiments are run on a personal computer with a 3.0 GHZ CPU and a 2.0 GB physical memory. We first report results on MNIST and USPS; we then present results on Chinese handwritten character database.

(a)

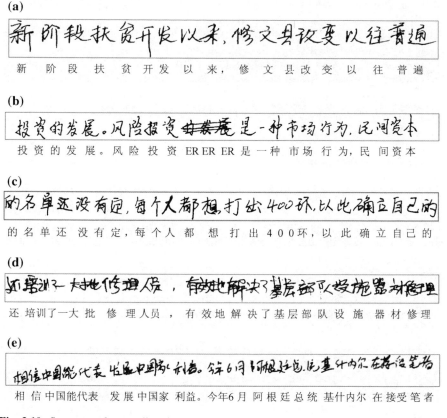

(b)

(c)

(d)

(e)

Fig. 3.10 Some complex text lines in test set which pose great challenges to the state-of-the-art segmentation-based systems. The ground truth of each text line is placed underneath. © [2007] IEEE. Reprinted, with permission, from Ref. (Su et al. 2007), **a** high-quality text line with long downward strokes and a little stroke overlapping, **b** text line with three instances of erasures (represented with ER), **c** text line with digit, punctuation, and Chinese characters, **d** text line with severe stroke touching, also with broken strokes, **e** text line with undulation and skewness

3.8.2.1 On Digit Databases

The error rates and training time of Perceptron learning (PL-MQDF) are given in Tables 3.1 and 3.2 with $k = 30$. We try active set technique in two different ways. For one trial (PL-2AS), we construct two active sets exactly following Sect. 3.4 and we set $\{N_1 = 1, N_2 = 3\}$. For the other (PL-1AS), we just generate one active set by simple using $\{N_1 = 10, N_2 = 0\}$. We also take efforts to train the MQDF using MCE criteria as in Liu et al. (2004). A speedup trick is employed for MCE-MQDF. We first compute the distance differences as in Eq. (3.7) for all training samples using the initial MQDF parameters and their average are taken as a threshold. During MCE training, if the squared distance from x to ω_r is bigger than that from x to ω_c by above threshold, SGD step is bypassed. For a close

Table 3.1 Error rates (%) and training time (s) on fine image features of MNIST database

Classifiers	*img*(400D)		*pca80*(80D)		*e-grg* (200D)	
	Err	CPU	Err	CPU	Err	CPU
MQDF	4.17	–	4.07	–	0.94	–
PL	1.55	238.98	1.52	84.94	0.52	129.84
PL-2AS	1.52	136.92	1.58	25.66	0.54	44.09
PL-1AS	1.51	122.55	1.49	22.70	0.53	30.61
MCE	1.92	196.28	1.80	79.75	0.53	119.91

© [2011] IEEE. Reprinted, with permission, from Ref. (Su et al. 2011)

Table 3.2 Error rates (%) and training time (s) on fine image features of USPS database

Classifiers	*img*(256D)		*e-grg* (128D)	
	Err	CPU	Err	CPU
MQDF	5.03	–	2.84	–
PL	3.94	21.63	2.19	14.80
PL-2AS	3.84	13.39	2.19	5.00
PL-1AS	3.94	12.00	2.24	3.55
MCE	4.09	15.69	2.49	22.39

© [2011] IEEE. Reprinted, with permission, from Ref. (Su et al. 2011)

comparison, we illustrate the error rates on each class in Figs. 3.11 and 3.12. PL-MQDF outperforms MCE-MQDF on both MNIST and USPS and there is no severe loss in accuracy by using active set technique. In terms of training time, both PL-1AS and PL-2AS bring great reduction. Consistently, PL-1AS works well with preferable performance.

The Effect of Sample Size. We select MNIST as a subject. We initially just draw 2,000 samples from training set, then increase the training volumes and evaluate the performance on test set. The results are given in Fig. 3.13. It shows that models using discriminative learning require more training samples for a robust learning.

3.8.2.2 On Chinese Character Database

Due to the heavy burden in computation consumption, discriminative learning algorithm is seldom attempted on large-category tasks. We will show that active set technique will speed up PL-MQDF greatly and render its usability on regular personal computers.

CASIA-HWDB1.0 and CASIA-HWDB1.1 are used to verify the efficacy of PL-MQDF. There are 3,755 classes (GB1 character set) and each class has about 570 training instances. We have 21,44,749 training samples and 5,33,675 test samples. As recommended in Liu et al. (2010), pseudo 2D LDI normalization is first executed and then NCGF features are extracted on gray-scale samples. Also,

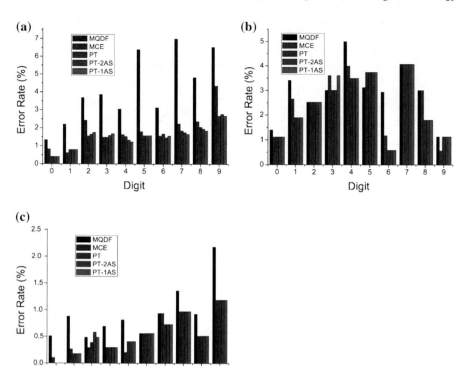

Fig. 3.11 The error rates per class of different methods on MNIST. © [2011] IEEE. Reprinted, with permission, from Ref. (Su et al. 2011), **a** *img* of MNIST, **b** *pca80* of MNIST, **c** *e-grg* of MNIST

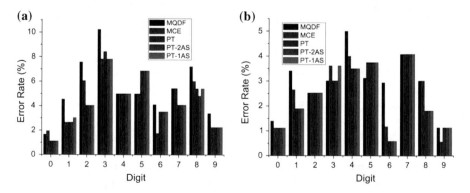

Fig. 3.12 The error rates per class of different methods on USPS. © [2011] IEEE. Reprinted, with permission, from Ref. (Su et al. 2011), **a** *img* of USPS, **b** *e-grg* of USPS

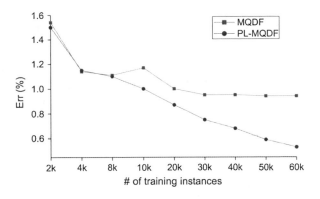

Fig. 3.13 Effect of training volumes for PL-MQDF (on e-grgof MNIST). © [2011] IEEE. Reprinted, with permission, from Ref. (Su et al. 2011)

LDA is employed to reduce the feature dimensionality from 512 to 160. In both experiments, we set $k = 50$.

We employ a two-stage classification process. In terms of testing, an LVQ classifier first ranks all classes and provides 100 candidate classes of leading rankings. Then quadratic models are incurred to re-rank the candidates and output the label of the first place. As for training process, training instances are cycled through repeatedly, and MQDF models are adjusted as needed. On each instance, LVQ classifier provides a candidate class set $\mathbf{M}$ ($|\mathbf{M}| = 10$ or $|\mathbf{M}| = 100$). If the true label of the instance is not included in $\mathbf{M}$, the SGD is bypassed. Otherwise, we only invoke SGD to update parameters each time violation of the margin constraint is found. We set $\rho = 0.05$ when dynamic margin is used, and we cycle 20 epochs through the training data (or active set).

The results are provided in Table 3.3. The MCE-MQDF is speeded up as mentioned in Sect. 3.8.2.1. We just summarize three general trends as follows. First, a small candidate set is enough for discriminative learning. There is at most 0.04 % extra error reduction from 100 candidate classes than 10; however, the time consumption is nearly doubled.

Table 3.3 Error rates (%) and training time (hour) on CASIA-HWDB1.0 and CASIA-HWDB1.1 databases

Classifiers(ρ)	$|\mathbf{M}| = 10$		$|\mathbf{M}| = 100$	
	Err	CPU	Err	CPU
MQDF	7.95	–	7.95	–
PL(0)	7.93	15.89	7.91	29.75
PL(0.05)	7.28	16.26	7.24	30.05
PL-1AS(0.05)	7.29	6.74	7.25	13.01
MCE	7.30	16.27	7.26	30.33

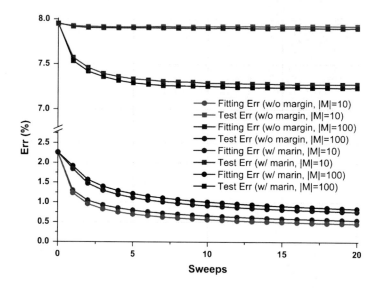

Fig. 3.14 Evaluation of PL-MQDF: the effect of candidate size and margin regularization. © [2011] IEEE. Reprinted, with permission, from Ref. (Su et al. 2011)

Second, regularization via margin is indispensable to PL-MQDF. It is easily stuck in overfitting solution without margin regularization and 8.20 % relative error reduction is yielded when $\rho = 0.05$. We plot the training process of PL-MQDF in Fig. 3.14.

Third, PL-MQDF is comparative to MCE-MQDF. In particular, our model requires lower computation cost when equipped with active set technique. The active set method accelerates PL-MQDF greatly, and the loss of accuracy is negligible. The ordered gains and losses w.r.t. all classes in accuracy are illustrated in Fig. 3.15. In all, the PL-MQDF achieves 8.30 % error reduction than MQDF with acceptable training cost.

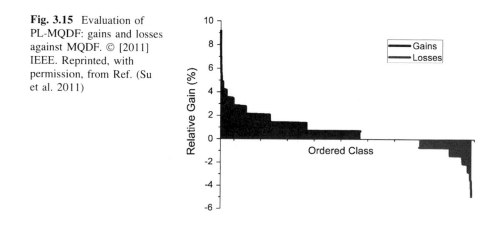

Fig. 3.15 Evaluation of PL-MQDF: gains and losses against MQDF. © [2011] IEEE. Reprinted, with permission, from Ref. (Su et al. 2011)

3.8.3 *Evaluation on HIT-MW Database*

The baseline systems are first tested on HIT-MW database for references. Then investigation on string-level training, synthesizing string samples, and linguistic correction are conducted.

3.8.3.1 Evaluation of Character Segmentation Approaches

Hong algorithm and Liu algorithm are evaluated in their character segmentation rates. The SCR results on digit, punctuation, and Chinese character are separately calculated and given in Table 3.4. In terms of SPR and SBR, their resultant is shown in Table 3.5.

From the above tables, Liu algorithm performs better than Hong algorithm in SCR, while the former performs worse than the latter in SPR. The reason can be partially found by investigating their SBR. The sign of the SBR can mostly reflect the tendency in under-segmentation and over-segmentation and its absolute value encodes the degree of the tendency. It seems that the segmentation results of Hong algorithm include severe under-segmentation and opposite effect observed in Liu algorithm.

3.8.3.2 Evaluation of Segmentation-Based Baseline Systems

Six systems in this framework are briefly evaluated. They follow different experimental setup. Their recognition results on HIT-MW database are shown in Table 3.6. These systems are named range from MQDF3-1 to MQDF3-6. The character segmentation approach is listed in parentheses. Techniques used in MQDF3-1 include sine aspect ratio, nonlinear shape normalization proposed by Tsukumo and Tamka, four plane feature (FPF), and MQDF3 classifier. MQDF3-2 applies additional Box-Cox feature transformation than MQDF3-1. For MQDF3-3 and MQDF3-4, Gradient features accompanying with blurring are used instead of

Table 3.4 Comparison of SCR (%)

	Digit	Punctuation	Chinese character	Average
Hong algorithm	16.96	21.59	65.67	60.26
Liu algorithm	40.00	44.44	74.23	70.51

Table 3.5 Comparison of SPR and SBR (%)

	SPR	SBR
Hong algorithm	71.27	−15.45
Liu algorithm	63.13	10.89

Table 3.6 The recognition rates of MQDF3-based systems

	DI (%)		PU (%)		CH (%)		Avg (%)	
	CR	AR	CR	AR	CR	AR	CR	AR
MQDF3-1 (Hong)	13.91	10.44	13.01	10.99	29.05	26.43	27.11	24.53
MQDF3-2 (Hong)	17.83	14.35	14.02	11.11	38.36	35.98	35.49	33.03
MQDF3-3 (Hong)	18.70	12.61	16.79	14.14	44.53	42.09	41.23	38.67
MQDF3-4 (Liu)	37.83	−5.22	39.14	18.06	50.69	37.66	49.25	34.65
MQDF3-5 (Hong)	19.13	13.48	14.39	9.85	49.27	47.20	45.18	42.78
MQDF3-6 (Liu)	37.39	−19.13	31.57	6.94	54.06	41.77	51.49	36.84

FPF features in MQDF3-2. Furthermore, to form MQDF3-5 and MQDF3-6, linear discriminant analysis (LDA) is added to MQDF-3 and MQDF-4. From the table, the effectiveness of blurring, Box-Cox transformation, and LDA are manifested.

3.8.3.3 Evaluation of Integrated Segmentation-Recognition Baseline System

An integrated segmentation-recognition baseline system is evaluated. The over-segmentation step employs the Liu algorithm. Then each segment is normalized using nonlinear shape normalization proposed by Tsukumo and Tamka. For feature extraction, Gradient features with blurring are used. MQDF2 is used to provide confidence information and it is trained on HCL2000 (400 sets) plus the training set of HIT-MW database. This classifier is utilized to verify the segmentation and recognition candidate lattice. Using Eq. (3.6), transcription of the text lines in test set can be given. The results are showed in Table 3.7.

3.8.3.4 Evaluation of String-Level Training

The isolated character samples from HCL2000 database (Zhang and Guo 2000) (400 sets) are used to train our baseline classifiers at the character level, and 1,142 handwritten string samples from the train and validation sets of HIT-MW database are used to update the parameters of the classifier at the string level. To ensure that the performance improvement resulted from the string-level training, we extract character samples composing the 1,142 string samples and add them into the character-level training set. So, our character training set contains 3,755 classes

Table 3.7 The evaluation of integrated segmentation-recognition baseline system

SCR (%)	DI (%)		PU (%)		CH (%)		Avg (%)	
	CR	AR	CR	AR	CR	AR	CR	AR
78.80	20.87	−13.91	13.40	−7.58	66.43	49.55	60.03	42.27

	SCR	CR
Character level	78.80	60.03
String level	79.42	61.90

Table 3.8 The evaluation of string level training (%)

with at least 400 samples per class and other 89 classes from the HIT-MW database, some of which only has one sample. Our evaluation is performed on a test set of the HIT-MW database, which contains 383 text lines (8,448 characters in total).

We compare the performance of character-level trained classifier and that of string-level trained classifier without synthetic samples. The parameters of classifier trained at character level serve as initialization for string-level training and are updated on the 1,142 natural string samples. The recognition results of the baseline classifier and updated classifier are listed in Table 3.8. From the table, we can see that the string-level training improves the CR by 1.87 %, while the SCR is improved by 0.62 %. Those results are got at the 72nd pass (we merely stop the process after 80 passes). We will later see that the curve may exceed this point (CR and SCR may be improved further), if more passes are used.

3.8.3.5 Evaluation of Synthetic Samples and Linguistic Constraints

First, we add the isolated characters composing the synthetic string samples into the character-level training set. Figure 3.16 shows the CRs of baseline classifiers and the corresponding copies of synthetic samples. The best rate 61.53 % (increased from 60.03 %) occurred when synthesizing 4 samples for each natural sample.

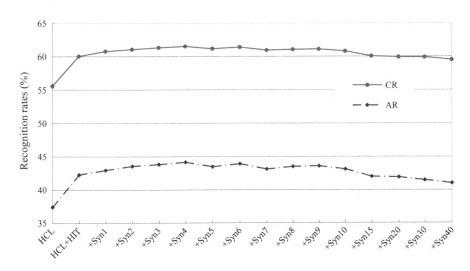

Fig. 3.16 Recognition rates of baseline classifiers

Fig. 3.17 The string-level
training process on expanded
training samples. © [2010]
IEEE. Reprinted, with
permission, from Ref.
(Chen et al. 2010)

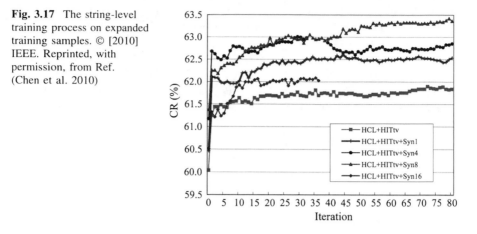

Then, we investigate the convergence speed of stochastic gradient descent in
Fig. 3.17. It can be seen that expanding the training set by synthetic string samples
improves the CR to 63.42 %, which is achieved using eight copies of synthetic
string samples at the 79th pass (denoted as HCL + HITtv + Syn8). However, the
results of HCL + HITtv + Syn1 and HCL + HITtv + Syn16 are slightly worse.
The former mainly suffers from the shortage of string samples, while the latter
makes the classifier bias to the unnatural styles.

In addition, to validate the quality of synthetic samples, we substitute all the
1,142 natural samples with one copy synthetic samples and measure its performance. It yields 60.23 % in CR and 78.88 % in SCR, comparable to the results of
using natural samples (60.03 % in CR and 78.80 % in SCR).

Finally, we briefly report the results on the utilization of bigram language. The
language model is derived from People's Daily corpus with 79,50,9778 characters.
If we synthesize 8 copies of string samples for training, the CR and AR are 61.38
and 43.96 %, respectively. Incorporating bigram language, the CR and AR have
increased to 76.54 and 58.14 % accordingly.

3.9 Conclusions

This chapter addresses the realistic Chinese handwriting recognition problem
using integrated segmentation-recognition strategy. Two kinds of reference systems are first described. One is segmentation-based system and the other is integrated segmentation-recognition baseline system. Analysis on them provides a
good starting point.

Sophisticated algorithms are utilized to improve the recognition accuracy or
reduce the training cost. For better generalization performance, dynamic margin
regularization is proposed within Perceptron learning. To relieve the heavy burden
in training process, we train the MQDF classifier using active set technique.

Moreover, string-level training also is utilized to adjust the initial MQDF on synthetic string samples. The learning process is directed by the MCE criterion. For linguistic contexts, a bigram language model is utilized to determine the segmentation and recognition process. Through experiments both on isolated character databases and on standard Chinese handwriting database, the efficacy of these algorithms is verified.

The aim of this chapter is not to be comprehensive, but simply to illustrate the various directions that improvement can take. There are many other effective approaches, such as confidence transformation, geometric modeling, which cannot be coved due to space limitation.

References

H. Baird, The state of the art of document image degradation modeling, in *DAS*, (2000)

C. Burges, O. Matan, Y. Le Cun, J.S. Denker, L.D. Jackel, C.E. Stenard, C.R. Nohl, J.I. Ben, Shortest path segmentation: a method for training a neural network to recognize character strings, in *Proceeding of IJCNN*. pp. 165–172, (1992)

X. Chen, T.-H. Su, T.-W. Zhang, Discriminative training of MQDF classifier on synthetic Chinese string samples, in *Chinese Conference on Patten Recognition (CCPR)*, (2010)

C.C. Cheng, F. Sha, L.K. Saul, A fast online algorithm for large margin training of continuous density Hidden Markov Models, in *Proceedings of Interspeech*. pp. 668–671, (2009)

M. Cheriet, N. Kharma, C.-L. Liu, C.Y. Suen, *Character recognition systems: a guide for students and practitioners* (Wiley, New Jersey, 2007)

K. Crammer, R. Gilad-Bachrach, A. Navot, Margin analysis of the LVQ algorithm, in *NIPS*, (2002)

R.O. Duda, P.E. Hart, D.G. Stork, *Pattern classification*, 2nd edn. (Wiley, New York, 2001)

H. Fujisawa, Forty years of research in character and document recognition: an industrial perspective. Pattern Recogn. **41**(8), 2435–2446 (2008)

H. Fujisawa, Y. Nakano, K. Kurino, Segmentation methods for character recognition: from segmentation to document structure analysis. Proc. IEEE **80**(7):1079–1092 (1992). doi:10.1109/5.156471

Guerfali W, Plamondon R, The delta log-normal theory for the generation and modeling of cursive characters. In: *ICDAR*. pp. 495–498, (1995)

R.V.D. Heiden, F.C.A. Groen, The Box-Cox metric for nearest neighbour classification improvement. Pattern Recogn. **30**(2), 273–279 (1997)

C. Hong, G. Loudon, Y. Wu, R. Zitserman, Segmentation and recognition of continuous handwriting Chinese text. Int. J. Pattern Recognit. Artif. Intell. **12**(2), 223–232 (1998)

T. Iijima, H. Genchi, K. Mori, A theoretical study of pattern identification by matching method, in *Proceedings of the 1st USA-JAPAN Computer Conference*, Tokyo, Japan. pp. 42–48, (1972)

X.-B. Jin, C.-L. Liu, X.-W. Hou, Regularized margin-based conditional log-likelihood loss for prototype learning. Pattern Recogn. **43**(7), 2428–2438 (2010)

B.-H. Juang, W. Chou, C.-H. Lee, Minimum classification error rate methods for speech recognition. IEEE Trans. Speech Audio Process. **5**(3), 257–265 (1997)

S.M. Katz, Estimation of probabilities from sparse data for the language model component of a speech recogniser. IEEE Trans. Acoust. Speech Signal Process. **35**(3), 400–401 (1987)

F. Kimura, K. Takashina, S. Tsuruoka, Y. Miyake, Modified quadratic discriminant functions and the application to Chinese character recognition. IEEE Trans. Pattern Anal. Mach. Intell. **9**(1), 149–153 (1987)

M. Kokula, Automatic generation of script font ligatures based on curve smoothness optimization. Electron Publ. **7**(4), 217–229 (1994)

K.-C. Leung, C.-H. Leung, Recognition of handwritten Chinese characters by combining regularization, fisher's discriminant and distorted sample generation, in *ICDAR*. pp. 1026–1030, (2009)

C.-L. Liu, Normalization-cooperated gradient feature extraction for handwritten character recognition. IEEE Trans. Pattern Anal. Mach. Intell. **29**(8), 1465–1469 (2007)

C.-L. Liu, M. Koga, H. Fujisawa, Lexicon-driven segmentation and recognition of handwritten character strings for Japanese address reading. IEEE Trans. Pattern Anal. Mach. Intell. **24**(11), 1425–1437 (2002)

C.-L. Liu, K. Nakashima, H. Sako, H. Fujisawa, Handwritten digit recognition: benchmarking of state-of-the-art techniques. Pattern Recogn. **36**(10), 2271–2285 (2003)

C.-L. Liu, H. Sako, H. Fujisawa, Discriminative learning quadratic discriminant function for handwriting recognition. IEEE Trans. Neural Netw. **15**(2), 430–444 (2004)

C.-L. Liu, F. Yin, D.-H. Wang, Q.-F. Wang, Online and offline handwritten Chinese character recognition: benchmarking on new databases, in *CJKPR*, (2010)

C.-L. Liu, F. Yin, D.-H. Wang, Q.-F. Wang, CASIA Online and Offline Chinese Handwriting Databases, in *International Conference on Document Analysis and Recognition*, pp. 37–41, (2011)

C.L. Liu, M. Katsumi, Handwritten numeral string recognition: character-level vs. string-level classifier training, in *Proceedings of the 17th International Conference on Pattern Recognition* (2004)

H. Liu, X Ding, Handwritten character recognition using gradient feature and quadratic classifier with multiple discrimination schemes, in *ICDAR* pp. 19–25, (2005)

M. Mori, A. Suzuki, A. Shio, S. Ohtsuka, Generating new samples from handwritten numerals based on point correspondence, in *IWFHR*. pp. 281–290, (2000)

Panagiotakopoulos C, Tsampouka P, The margin perceptron with unlearning, in *ICML*, (2010)

F. Rosenblatt, The perceptron: A probabilistic model for information storage and organization in the brain. Psychol. Rev. **65**(6), 386–408 (1958)

T.-H. Su, C.-L. Liu, X.-Y. Zhang, Perceptron Learning of Modified Quadratic Discriminant Function, in *International Conference on Document Analysis and Recognition*, (2011)

T.-H. Su, T.-W. Zhang, D.-J. Guan, Off-line Recognition of Realistic Chinese Handwriting Using Segmentation-free Strategy. Pattern Recogn. **42**(1), 167–182 (2009)

T.-H. Su, T.-W. Zhang, H.-J. Huang, Y. Zhou, HMM-based recognizer with segmentation-free strategy for unconstrained Chinese handwritten text, in *International Conference on Document Analysis and Recognition. IEEE*, pp. 133–137, (2007)

J. Tsukumo, H. Tanaka, Classification of handprinted Chinese characters using non-linear normalization and correlation methods, in *Proceedings of the 9th International Conference on Pattern Recognition*, Rome, Italy, pp. 168–171, (1988)

Varga T, Off-line cursive handwriting recognition using synthetic training data. PhD Thesis, University of Bern, Bern, 2006

Q.-F. Wang, F. Yin, C.-L. Liu, Integrating Language Model in Handwritten Chinese Text Recognition, in *International Conference on Document Analysis and Recognition*, pp. 1036–1040, (2009)

Y. Wang, Q. Huo, Sample-separation-margin based minimum classification error training of pattern classifiers with quadratic discriminant functions, in *IEEE International Conference on Acoustics, Speech and Signal Processing. IEEE*, pp. 1866–1869, (2010)

H. Zhang, J. Guo, Introduction to HCL2000 database, in *Proceedings of Sino-Japan Symposium on Intelligent Information Networks*, Beijing, (2000)

Chapter 4
Segmentation-Free Strategy: Basic Algorithms

Abstract The off-line recognition of realistic Chinese handwriting poses significant challenges. This chapter presents a baseline system for a HMMs-based, segmentation-free strategy to address this problem, in which the character segmentation stage is avoided prior to recognition. Handwritten text lines are first converted to observation sequences using sliding windows. Then an embedded Baum-Welch algorithm is used to train character HMMs. Finally, a posterior best character string maximizing is performed with the help of the Viterbi algorithm. Experiments are conducted on the HIT-MW database, which includes data from more than 780 writers. The results show the feasibility of such systems and reveal apparent complementary capacities between the segmentation-free systems and the segmentation-based ones.

4.1 Introduction

This chapter attempts to recognize Chinese handwriting with a large vocabulary from segmentation-free strategy. This investigation is motivated by the following observations:

- Low expenditure in preparation of training data. Labeling each character in training data, which is a tedious and time-consuming process, is passed by in segmentation-free systems. In the segmentation-free strategy, we only input the text lines and their underlying character string. The system automatically aligns each character to its image counterpart and then estimates the model of that character. It simplifies the expansion of training data as well as quickens the experimental process.
- Desirable features of different origins. Segmentation-free systems usually adopt sliding windows moving along the text line without regard to the boundary of underlying characters, while segmentation-based ones extract features within

T. Su, *Chinese Handwriting Recognition: An Algorithmic Perspective*,
SpringerBriefs in Electrical and Computer Engineering,
DOI: 10.1007/978-3-642-31812-2_4, © The Author(s) 2013

each character segment. Their different origins result in different abilities in characterizing the character pattern, which plays important role in the system combination. For example, segmentation-based systems can express the certain class more elaborately, especially in vertical direction; segmentation-free ones can utilize the conjunction relationship between adjacent characters in a simple way.

- Intrinsic advantages of the strategy. Segmentation-free strategy performs character segmentation and recognition in one step, and outputs a best transcription in probabilistic criteria. Compared with the segmentation-based strategy, it can utilize both the boundary information of sliding windows and the knowledge of character models, and avoid the blind character segmentation. Moreover, due to its solid mathematic foundation and powerful dynamic capacity, HMM can properly absorb the writing variability (Koerich et al. 2005). In addition, language models can be incorporated conveniently (Marti and Bunke 2001; Vinciarelli et al. 2004).

- Extra options to multiple classifier combination research. Given the huge challenges in the recognition of Chinese handwriting, as in the English word recognition task, multiple classification methods or properly combining a variety of classifier outputs may be the future trends. Segmentation-free strategy is devised from overall different perspective to the segmentation-based one and may serve as a desirable complementary strategy.

This chapter is organized as follows. The next section briefly describes the baseline system. From Sect. 4.3 to Sect. 4.5, main components of our baseline system are detailed, including sliding window, feature extraction method, and HMM modeling. Experiments are conducted and results are summarized in Sect. 4.6.

4.2 System Overview

When a text line image is fed into a recognizer, it is converted to a sequence of feature vectors or observations $\mathbf{O} = \mathbf{o}_1, \ldots, \mathbf{o}_m$. The recognition task is to identify a string of characters $S' = s_1, \ldots, s_n$ maximizing the a posteriori (MAP) $P(S|\mathbf{O})$. The recognizer described in this chapter consists of three main components: sliding window, feature extraction and selection, HMM training and decoding. The baseline system architecture is illustrated in Fig. 4.1.

4.3 Sliding Windowing

Windowing is a common localization technique in signal processing domain. Since the character string runs in certain direction, a movable window called

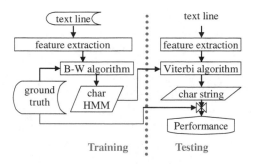

Fig. 4.1 Basic architecture for HMMs-based segmentation-free systems. The ground truth database is the reference text of text line database, and it is used not only in the training stage but also in the performance evaluation stage; the character HMMs are generated by embedded Baum-Welch algorithm (B-W algorithm) on training and validation sets after the sliding window-based feature selection stage; using Viterbi algorithm, the test set is mapped into the symbol space

sliding window following the same order can be used to draw an interested zone and then extract features within it. Generally, the height of the sliding window is the same as that of text line. The other two parameters, the width W and the shift step S, should be assigned by researchers or determined through experiments. Supposing $f(p, q)$ is the digital image of a text line, the running mechanism of the sliding window is illustrated in Fig. 4.2. The window function can be expressed as

$$g(w, v) = \begin{cases} 1, & w = 1, \ldots, W \\ 0 & \text{otherwise.} \end{cases} \tag{4.1}$$

Then the window at step i can be denoted as:

$$f_i = f((i-1)S + w, v) \cdot g(w, v), \tag{4.2}$$

where $\cdot$ is the multiplication operator. The feature vector at step i, $\mathbf{o}_i$, in observation sequence $\mathbf{O} = \mathbf{o}_1, \ldots, \mathbf{o}_m$ is calculated as follows:

$$\mathbf{o}_i = \psi(f_i), \tag{4.3}$$

where ψ is the feature mapping function from image space to feature space.

Fig. 4.2 Feature selection process using sliding window. (W–S) columns are shared between adjacent windows in ith step and ($i + 1$)th step (marked with *solid* and *dashed lines*, respectively)

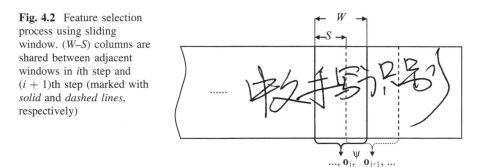

The sliding window used in Refs. (Marti and Bunke 2001); (Mohamed and Gader 1996) is of one pixel width and one pixel step. There is no overlap between adjacent windows. Another kind of sliding window with step of one pixel and width of 10 pixels is given in Ref. (Vinciarelli et al. 2004). Obviously, nine-tenth contents of two consecutive windows are identical. In addition, (Natarajan et al. 2001) presents a bit adaptive sliding window relative to the height of text line: the width is of one-fifteenth its height and the step of one-third its width. This book sets $W = 12$ pixels (one-fifth the character's average width) and $S = 2$ pixels (one-sixth its width). The window width W is selected to make a balance between the HMM structure and the smallest character width, and the tuning process of window step S is detailed in Ref. (Su et al. 2007b).

4.4 Feature Representation

A distinctive and compact representation of patterns is the key aim of feature extraction and selection. We employ a sliding window moving horizontally on a text line to draw an interesting zone and then map image space to feature space. To resist the undulation of text lines, we partition the window into three zones, as shown in Fig. 4.3 and only the body zone is used to extract feature vector instead of the whole window. The body zone is separated by the topmost and bottommost foreground pixels in vertical direction.

Our baseline system is based on cell features. The window is divided into 8×2 cells, and then the foreground pixels are summed in each cell. We also adapt another feature representation method, FPF (Chen et al. 1997), which is originally used in Chinese isolated-character recognition. Each character image is scanned in four directions (horizontal, vertical, right diagonal and left diagonal) and only the strokes longer than a threshold are retained. Then each plane is divided into cells within which stroke crossing can be counted. Some modifications of the original algorithm are needed to fit the problem of handwriting recognition: (1) the feature vector is extracted from certain sliding window instead of character segment; (2) the average stroke width SW is estimated on whole text line by the analysis of stroke histogram (Cf. Sect. 2.4.4) rather than on single character by contour following; (3) the four planes are formed by excluding the strokes smaller than

Fig. 4.3 The zone used to extract features. The blank parts in the *upper* and *lower* window are excluded

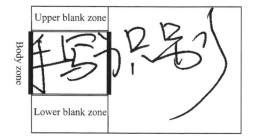

$2 \times SW$. We use this 64-dimensional feature vector in this book to improve the performance of the baseline system. Figure 4.4 shows the extraction process of FPFs. Further, we incorporate the previous two features as an extended 80-dimensional feature vector to enhance the recognizer.

In addition, principal component analysis (PCA) is adopted. The covariance matrix is calculated from train and validation sets and 36 out of 80 principal components are retained according to the criteria declared in Ref. (Rencher 2002) as a compact representation of previous mentioned 80-dimensional fused features. Further information in this aspect is available in Ref. (Su et al. 2007a).

4.5 HMM Training and Decoding

Supposing the sequence of feature vectors corresponding to handwritten text line is $\mathbf{O} = \mathbf{o}_1, \ldots, \mathbf{o}_m$, the task of the recognizer is to identify a character string:

$$S' = \arg \max_S P(S|O). \tag{4.4}$$

Using Bayes' theorem, we get:

$$S' = \arg \max_S \frac{P(O|S)P(S)}{P(\mathbf{O})}. \tag{4.5}$$

Since $P(\mathbf{O})$ is the a priori of feature vectors and independent of S, above equation is equivalent to:

$$S' = \arg \max_S P(O|S)P(S). \tag{4.6}$$

We call $P(O|S)$ the string model and $P(S)$ the language model. The former encodes the probability of feature vectors $\mathbf{O}$ under character string S and the latter constrains the search space. Provided that $\mathbf{O}$ is of conditional independence, $P(O|S)$ can be further approximated as:

$$P(O|S) \approx \prod_{i=1}^n P(\mathbf{O}_i|s_i), \tag{4.7}$$

where $\mathbf{O}_i$ is the observations of character s_i. The $P(\mathbf{O}_i|s_i)$ is the character HMM and estimated by embedded Baum-Welch algorithm. When $P(O|S)$ and $P(S)$ are in order, the best character string in the MAP sense (as in Eq. 4.6) can be located by Viterbi algorithm (Rabiner 1989). Note that the meaning of $\mathbf{O}_i$ is different from $\mathbf{o}_i$ in that $\mathbf{o}_i$ is derived from certain sliding window and $\mathbf{O}_i$ is a series of $\mathbf{o}_i$ which is the counterpart of a character. Their relationship can be characterized as:

$$\mathbf{O} = \mathbf{o}_1, \ldots, \mathbf{o}_m = \mathbf{O}_1, \ldots, \mathbf{O}_n, \quad m \geq n. \tag{4.8}$$

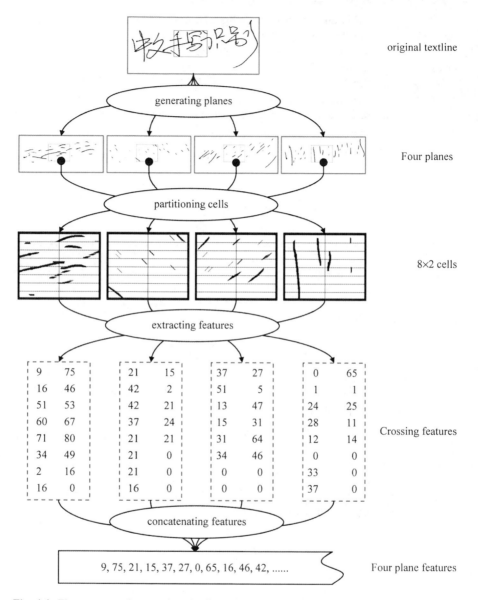

Fig. 4.4 The process of extracting 64-dimensional four plane features. The sliding window plotted here is larger than the actual size to give a clear illustration. Reprinted from Ref. Su et al. (2009), Copyright 2009, with permission from Elsevier

An HMM is an extended Markov chain. The transitions between states represent the shifts of character segments and each state of the chain associates a probability density spanned on a d-dimensional feature space. A continuous-density HMM (CDHMM) can be noted as $\lambda = (\mathbf{A}, B, \Pi)$. $\mathbf{A} = (a_{ij})$ is the state transition probability. $B = \{b_j(\mathbf{o})\}$ is the observation probability. Further, the probability of observation $\mathbf{o}$ for state j, $b_j(\mathbf{o})$, can be approximated by a finite mixture of Gaussian density of the form:

$$b_j(\mathbf{o}) = \sum c_{jk}\Omega\left(\mathbf{o}, \mu_{jk,}\Sigma_{ij}\right), \quad 1 \le j \le N, \tag{4.9}$$

where N is the total states, $\mathbf{o}$ a d-dimensional vector, c_{jk} the mixture coefficient and μ_{jk}, Σ_{jk} the mean vector and covariance matrix for Gaussian distribution Ω, respectively. Π is the initial parameter set concerning the HMM topography, mean vector, and covariance matrix in each state, mixture coefficients, etc.

Our recognizer models each Chinese character class as an 11-state CDHMM, while a four-state CDHMM is given to the character class in digit or punctuation. The structure of the HMM is a Bakis form (left-to-right, with no skip). The initialization of parameters $\mathbf{A}$ and B, is done by a flat start. Before detail the technique aspect of embedded Baum-Welch algorithm, we visualize the key factors and explain their roles in the training process as shown in Fig. 4.5. To simplify the expression, one entry state and one exit state are added to each character HMM. However, output probability is not associated to them. From Fig. 4.5, we can see that character HMMs are embedded in sentence HMMs. The parameter set of sentence HMM is updated during training and the character HMMs in the sentence HMM will be renewed simultaneously.

Once the initialization of λ's is done, the embedded HMMs are reestimated by embedded Baum-Welch algorithm, which uses a maximum likelihood (ML) criterion. Suppose the training data (sequence of text line observations) is denoted as

Fig. 4.5 The factors in the running process of embedded Baum-Welch algorithm. Handwritten text line is first mapped to text line observations by feature extraction function. Character HMMs are often coarsely initialized and concatenated to form the sentence HMM at the guidance of text line label. As the last step, embedded Baum-Welch algorithm will update the character HMMs using text line observations. Reprinted from Ref. Su et al. (2009), Copyright 2009, with permission from Elsevier

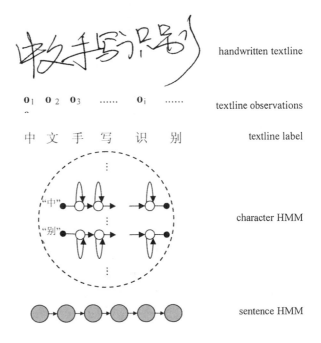

$\mathbf{O}^r$ ($1 \leq r \leq R$), and N_q is the number of states of the qth HMM in a certain sentence HMM. The objective function used by ML training is as follows (Gales and Young 2007):

$$L_{\mathrm{ML}}(\lambda) = \sum_{r=1}^{R} \log p_\lambda(\mathbf{O}^r|S^r), \tag{4.10}$$

where S^r is the ground truth of the rth text line feature observation $\mathbf{O}^r$. As the estimation of output distribution can be easily derived from the estimation formula of Baum-Welch algorithm (Rabiner 1989), we only provide the reestimation of transition matrix as follows:

$$\hat{a}_{ij}^{(q)} = \frac{\sum_{r=1}^{R} (1/P_r) \sum_{t=1}^{T_r-1} \alpha_i^{(q)r}(t) a_{ij}^{(q)} b_j^{(q)}(\mathbf{o}_{t+1}^r) \beta_j^{(q)r}(t+1)}{\sum_{r=1}^{R} (1/P_r) \sum_{t=1}^{T_r} \alpha_i^{(q)r}(t) \beta_j^{(q)r}(t)}, \tag{4.11}$$

$$(i \neq 1, j \neq N_q)$$

where P_r is the probability of the rth observation, and $\alpha_i^{(q)r}(t)$, $\beta_j^{(q)r}(t+1)$ are the forward and backward probability, respectively. The transition updating of entry state and exit state is trivial and omitted here.

The forward probability at time t, $\alpha_j^{(q)r}(t)$ can be calculated in a recursive way:

$$a_j^{(q)r}(t) = \left[\alpha_1^{(q)r}(t) a_{1j}^{(q)} + \sum_{i=2}^{N_q-1} \alpha_i^{(q)r}(t-1) a_{ij}^{(q)} \right] b_j^{(q)}(\mathbf{o}_t^r). \tag{4.12}$$

$$(t > 1, j \neq 1, j \neq Nq)$$

Similarly, backward probability can be expressed.

In the recognition phase, the character models are concatenated to strings (Vinciarelli et al. 2004) in this chapter there is no extra language information incorporated yet. Since any character can occur at any position, a string network can be formed. The best path is found out through Viterbi algorithm by a MAP criterion (Rabiner 1989). This phase actually maps the text line image to a character string (see Fig. 4.6). There is no explicit segmentation of the text line into characters, though the soft segmentation is delivered as a by-product in recognition phase.

4.6 Experiments

In this section, the baseline system is tested on a subset of HIT-MW database (Cf. Sect. 3.8.1). Evaluations are provided in the next two subsections. Finally, a brief discussion is given in Sect. 4.6.3.

Fig. 4.6 Recognition
process is to map features to
symbols. Here, h_n is the
history of s

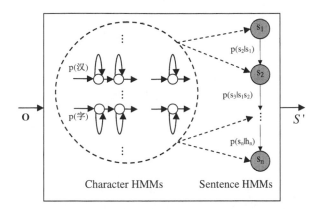

4.6.1 Evaluation on Segmentation-Free Systems

In our recognizer, an HMM per character is given and all erasures (three erasures
are presented in the second line of Fig. 3.10) are modeled as one HMM. In
addition, to model the large space between characters, we add a "blank" HMM.
Eventually, there are 2075 character models. The results are counted excluding
English letters, due to their too limited occurrences in Chinese environment
(13 letters with only 20 instances in all).

We use an incremental way to explore the features for the segmentation-free
systems. As mentioned previously, the baseline system uses a 16-dimensional
feature vector, which is derived from cell features (labeled as 16DCELL). Then
we replace the 16-dimensional cell features with 64-dimensional FPFs,
80-dimensional fused features (the corresponding systems are denoted as 64DFPF,
80DFUS, respectively) to study the effect of different features. Moreover, a
dimension reduction process by PCA is evaluated (the system is labeled as 36DPCA).
Finally, a grand variance tying method (refereed as 36DGVS) which is originally
used in speech recognition is taken into consideration. Grand variance system is a
typical data sharing method to alleviate the data insufficiency and it means that all
HMMs share the same Gaussian variance. When reestimating the variance, training
data which would have been used for each of original unshared variance are
deposited. As a result, more reliable estimation of Gaussian density can be obtained.

Due to their distinct differences in shape, the results of digit, punctuation, and
Chinese character by the segmentation-free systems are separately evaluated and
are summarized in Table 4.1. The maximal and minimal items in each row are
highlighted with Δ and ∇, respectively. Seen from Table 4.1, no system achieves
the best or worst *CR* and *AR* simultaneously.

We first consider the average recognition rates. It is clear that a noticeable
improvement has been achieved after incremental enhancement. The *CR* and *AR*
have increased from 33.54 and 29.18 % (of baseline system) to 44.22 and 39.08 %
(of 36DGVS), respectively. Both promotions account for about 10 %. Among such
segmentation-free systems, the smallest two promotions are laid in the *CR* of

Table 4.1 The recognition rates of different systems evaluated on test set (CH, DI, and PU are the acronyms of Chinese characters, digit and punctuation, respectively)

	DI (%)		PU (%)		CH (%)		Average (%)	
	CR	AR	CR	AR	CR	AR	CR	AR
16DCELL	42.61(∇)	36.09	29.17(Δ)	25.38(Δ)	33.76(∇)	29.47(∇)	33.57(∇)	29.26(∇)
64DFPF	44.35	36.52	19.32	16.16	35.29	32.57	34.04	31.14
80DFUS	57.39(Δ)	39.13	27.63	22.69	36.67	32.61	36.38	31.85
36DPCA	56.96	46.09(Δ)	28.14	17.36	39.59	35.33	38.97	33.93
36DGVS	52.17	35.22(∇)	5.58(∇)	4.18(∇)	48.22(Δ)	43.03(Δ)	44.334(Δ)	39.184(Δ)

64DFPF and the *AR* of 80DFUS. Using Wilcoxon signed-rank test in (Freund 1984), their statistical significance holds at 0.16 and 0.09 levels, respectively. Other improvements are all statistically significant with confidence more than 99 %.

Further, we consider the digit recognition. As for *CR*, 16DCELL is the lowest one. The performance of 64DFPF in this respect outperforms 16DCELL. The 80DFUS reaches the best *CR* by the fusion of cell features and FPFs. The *CR*s of 36DPCA and 36DGVS drop down in turn. Similar trend can be observed in their *AR* performances. However, a mass of insertions occur in digit, and 80DFUS and 36DGVS are the two systems that suffered most due to this problem. As a result, 80DFUS does not reach the maximum while 36DGVS reaches the minimum (Table 4.1).

The best performance is demonstrated in 16DCELL when identifying the punctuation. The results of 64DFPF are inferior to 16DCELL. The feature fusion, dimension reduction, and variance sharing techniques present no improvement at all in recognition rates, and a sharp decrease in *CR* and *AR* can be easily observed relating to 36DGVS.

Unlike the punctuation recognition, almost all enhancement operations increase the performance with regard to the Chinese character recognition. The best performance is achieved by 36DGVS and the worst is by 16DCELL.

We proceed to analyze the error distribution of the segmentation-free systems. Three types of errors, delete error, insertion error, and substitute error, are separately considered to each system and the error ratios are summarized in Table 4.2 as regards to digit, punctuation, and Chinese characters, respectively. For example, the deletion errors of digit constitute 7.39 % of whole deletion errors. Among 8471 characters in test set, 2.72, 9.36, and 87.92 % are comprised by digit, punctuation, and Chinese character samples, respectively. Comparing 64DFPF with 16DCELL, obvious advantages are shown in characterizing the Chinese characters, seeing that all types of error ratios in Chinese characters are lower, while the opposite effect is observed in punctuation. On the fusion of FPFs and cell features (80DFUS), the insertion and the deletion error ratios in Chinese characters decrease. However, higher error ratios of insertion and deletion are occurred in digit and in punctuation, respectively. The small strokes of Chinese character are more likely to be

Table 4.2 The error ratios on test set between digit punctuation and Chinese character of segmentation-free systems. Reprinted from Su et al. (2009), Copyright 2009, with permission from Elsevier

	16DCELL (%)			64DFPF (%)			80DFUS (%)			36DPCA (%)			36DGVS (%)		
	DI	PU	CH	DI	PU	CH	DI	PU	CH	DI	PU	CH	DI	PU	CH
DE	7.39	17.43	75.18	5.47	19.50	75.03	5.35	20.36	74.29	5.65	20.68	73.67	6.00	37.67	56.33
IE	3.79	8.13	88.08	6.50	10.16	83.34	10.80	10.03	79.17	5.52	18.76	75.72	8.97	2.53	88.50
SE	1.62	8.95	89.43	1.64	10.00	88.36	1.31	9.26	89.43	1.41	9.71	88.88	1.49	10.82	87.69

misinterpreted as digit. On the contrary, punctuation tends to be viewed as a part of the neighboring Chinese character. The error ratios of Chinese character decrease from 80DFUS to 36DPCA. This finding verifies the positive role of PCA technique in the discriminative description of Chinese characters. As for 36DGVS, a remarkable reduction of deletion error ratio and substitution error ratio are observed in Chinese characters and as a result, a promising recognition rates are achieved in Table 4.1.

Above robustness is achieved at some loss of modeling precision. For example, the GVS gives a larger insertion error ratio than 36DPCA. The recognition results of the text lines in Fig. 3.10c and e are illustrated in Figs. 4.7 and 4.8, respectively. The correctly identified characters are underlined. As the character boundary can be obtained as a by-product of the recognition process, we plot it in the first row of each subfigure whose intensity expressing the probability in that position and the segments enclosed by two adjacent boundary lines are labeled with numbers. The boundary line is of the same width of the sliding window.

We can see that substitution errors often occur between similar characters. Two kinds of similar characters are clarified in (Liu 2008) due to their inherent similarity or distortion during writing process. The former is the main source of substitution errors. Such instances are marked with "S1" in Figs. 4.7 and 4.8. In cursive characters, substitutions often fall into the latter. Such cases are marked with "S2" in Figs. 4.7 and 4.8. The other substitution errors are mainly resulted from the precision of the HMMs. Moreover, we can see that the misidentified segments contribute to the deletion and insertion errors.

In addition, the noise resistance can be verified. Some outliers incurred from small stroke can be solved. Examples cast in this category are marked with "H1" in Figs. 4.7 and 4.8. Even unacceptable segments may be correctly identified (see the examples marked with "H2" in Figs. 4.7 and 4.8).

To establish a reliable inference in statistics, we only consider those characters whose sample size is over 20. Following points are observed. First, substitutions are often found between similar characters. Second, deletion is mainly occurred in digit and punctuation, as digit or punctuation is often mis-explained as a component of its neighboring Chinese character. Such digit and punctuation, whose deletion error rates are bigger than 1 %, include zero, comma, period, caesura sign, and left-double quotation mark. Last, insertion seems more dependent on system setup. Only the insertion error rate of the digit, "1", is consistently bigger than 1 % in all segmentation-free systems.

To sum up, it is preferable and important to design discriminative features and represent them properly. The cell features are sensitive to the stroke width but more suitable than FPFs to represent the punctuation. On the contrary, the FPF seems a good descriptor in characterizing the directional structures most presented in digits or Chinese characters. The fusion of above two kinds of features yields acceptable tradeoff or improvement of performance. The dimension reduction by PCA and variance sharing through GVS shows efficiencies in alleviating the insufficient training data. However, adverse effects are observed in the recognition of digits and punctuation.

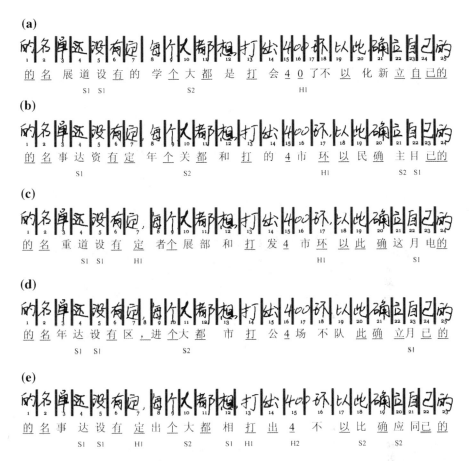

Fig. 4.7 Recognition results of the text line in Fig. 3.10c. *Upper* row of each subfigure shows the soft segmentation boundary imposed on the text line. *Middle* row of each subfigure is copied from the recognition result of the text line and the correctly recognized characters are underlined to give a clear view. *Lower* row of each subfigure highlights some segments and characters with S1 (substitute error is due to their inherent similarity), S2 (substitute error results from writing distortion), H1 (correctly identified segment with small outliers) and H2 (correctly identified block with large outliers). Reprinted from Ref. (Su et al. 2009), Copyright 2009, with permission from Elsevier (**a**) recognition results by 16DCELL (**b**) recognition results by 64DFPF (**c**) recognition results by 80DFUS (**d**) recognition results by 36DPCA (**e**) recognition results by 36DGVS

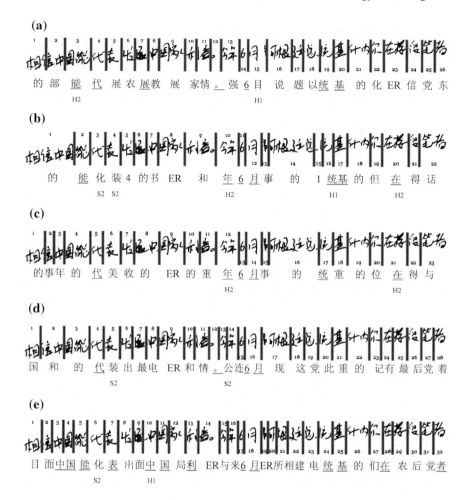

Fig. 4.8 Recognition results of the text line in Fig. 3.10e. *Upper* row of each subfigure shows the soft segmentation boundary imposed on the text line. *Middle* row of each subfigure is copied from the recognition result of the text line and the correctly recognized characters are underlined to give a clear view. *Lower* row of each subfigure highlights some segments and characters with S1 (substitute error is due to their inherent similarity), S2 (substitute error results from writing distortion), H1 (correctly identified segment with small outliers), and H2 (correctly identified block with large outliers). Reprinted from Su et al. (2009), Copyright 2009, with permission from Elsevier (**a**) recognition results by 16DCELL (**b**) recognition results by 64DFPF (**c**) recognition results by 80DFUS (**d**) recognition results by 36DPCA (**e**) recognition results by 36DGVS

4.6.2 Comparison Between Segmentation-Based and Segmentation-Free Systems

Two systems with MQDF3 classifier are experimented with the help of Hong's character segmentation algorithm (Hong et al. 1998) (Cf. Sect. 3.8.3.2 for more details). One of them (MQDF3-2) applies Box-Cox transformation in the feature extraction stage besides the combination of nonlinear normalization, adaptive aspect ratio. The power of the transformation is set to 0.5 intuitively. The other (MQDF3-1) is a baseline system which uses a similar setup but no Box-Cox transformation is applied. The parameters, k and i, are tuned on validation set with MQDF3-2, and it shows that the classification rate yields best when k and i are set to 7 and 1.7 times of the global variance. Their results are presented in Table 4.3. Following two points can be concluded:

(1) The recognition rates of MQDF3-1 are much lower than 80DFUS. As previous description of segmentation-free systems, neither shape normalization (including size scaling, nonlinear normalization, and elastic cell) nor variable transformation is exploited till now. Thus, it appears that HMM may properly model the stroke variability and the sliding window-based feature extraction method may encode appealing information between adjacent characters.

(2) MQDF3-2 yields a great improvement than MQDF3-1. Further compared with 80DFUS, obvious increments are observed in the recognition rates of Chinese character. Certainly, after three decades research on handwritten Chinese isolated-character recognition, there are many techniques available to improve the recognizers. However, 80DFUS manifests advantages in the recognition of digit and punctuation. This consideration pushes us to combine MQDF3-2 with 80DFUS.

We also report computational time and memory both on a desktop PC computer and a laptop. The description of computers is listed in Table 4.4. The average CPU

Table 4.3 The recognition rates of MQDF3-based systems on test set

	DI (%)		PU (%)		CH (%)		Avg (%)	
	CR	AR	CR	AR	CR	AR	CR	AR
MQDF3-1	13.91	10.44	13.01	10.99	29.05	26.43	27.11	24.53
MQDF3-2	17.83	14.35	14.02	11.11	38.36	35.98	35.49	33.03

Reprinted from Su et al. (2009), Copyright 2009, with permission from Elsevier

Table 4.4 Computers used to measure performance

	CPU				Memory (MB)
		Name	Alias	Clocks (GHZ)	
Desktop PC		Pentium 4	P68, Willamette	1.37	256
Laptop		Mobile Duo T5600	Merom-2M	1.79	1024

Table 4.5 Average CPU time consuming of segmentation-free systems (unit: ms/character)

	16DCELL	64DFPF	80DFUS	36DPCA	36DGVS	MQDF3-2
Character segmentation	–	–	–	–	–	1.14
						(0.37)
Feature extraction	24.52	155.02	169.72	171.71	171.17	346.53
	(8.23)	(41.29)	(45.30)	(46.36)	(46.36)	(106.53)
Recognition	1950.21	3599.86	5788.50	2272.52	4039.63	574.33
	(704.13)	(1514.28)	(1923.47)	(1089.20)	(1769.87)	(164.48)

The CPU time measured on laptop is given in parenthesis

time per character of segmentation-free and segmentation-based systems are separately given in Table 4.5. The former include the CPU time of feature extraction and that of recognition. As for the latter, the time of character segmentation is provided, too. To estimate the memory consumption of each recognizer, the storage size of character models is summarized in Table 4.6.

From Tables 4.5 to 4.6, following points can be inferred:

(1) The CPU time and memory needed by segmentation-free systems in this chapter are mainly dependent on their dimensionality of feature vector and the number of Gaussian mixtures; the 16DCELL (with five Gaussian mixtures) consumes smallest time and memory. With the increase of feature size, 64DFPF (also with five Gaussian mixtures) requires above double time and nearly quadruple storage. The 80DFUS (with six Gaussian mixtures) becomes the most intensive recognizer in time and storage consumptions. Once PCA is used, the overall time and storage are greatly saved in 36DPCA (with four Gaussian mixtures) though the time spent on feature extraction increases. More Gaussian mixtures are needed in 36DGVS (with eight Gaussian mixtures) when GVS is further adopted, which results in a bit more time consumption and a slight increase of storage. However, with an eye to the recognition rates, PCA and GVS are effective techniques to enhance the segmentation-free systems.

(2) Disadvantages in speed are observed in segmentation-free systems when compared with MQDF3-2. Among them, 80DFUS requires the most intensive CPU time and memory. In the next chapter, the integration of 80DFUS and MQDF3-2 provides improvement in average recognition rates, while it made a tradeoff between their CPU time.

Table 4.6 Memory consuming of segmentation-based and segmentation-free systems (unit: MB)

16DCELL	64DFPF	80DFUS	36DPCA	36DGVS	MQDF3
17.57	58.63	86.48	28.05	30.96	33.09

Fig. 4.9 The histogram of the number of samples. The data are derived from train and validation sets. Reprinted from Ref. Su et al. (2009), Copyright 2009, with permission from Elsevier

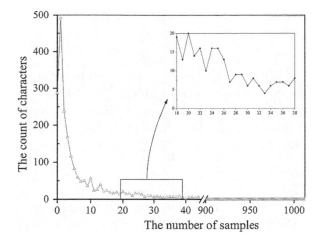

4.6.3 Discussions

The recognition rates of both segmentation-based systems and segmentation-free ones are no more than 50 %. The low rates are partially attributed to the complexities of the realistic handwriting. However, the data sparseness also has remarkable impact.

Data sparseness is a common problem in natural language processing. As soon as Chinese handwriting is concerned, a great deal of Chinese characters may occur few times ever never occur. In other words, many character models have insufficient training samples. As a result, robust parameter estimation is impossible and on the other hand the recognizer easily falls into "overfitting". This problem in alphabetic languages like English may be not as severe as in Chinese. In recognition systems for English text, they can model the letters instead of words and

Fig. 4.10 Relationship between the number of samples and *CR*. With the exponential increase in the number of samples, it shows proportional improvements in *CR*. Reprinted from Ref. Su et al. (2009), Copyright 2009, with permission from Elsevier

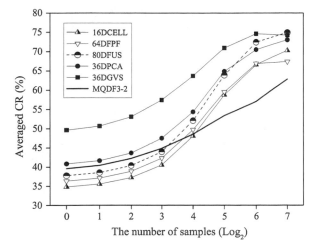

then arrange letter models to word model, since plenty of letters are available. Unfortunately, Chinese character is the basic writing unit, thus no straightforward way to condense the large number of models. We plot the distribution of the samples in Fig. 4.9. The coordinate (10, 56) means that there are 56 character class, which possess 10 samples in train and validation sets. Among them, 13.83 % have no training samples at all and 52.10 % possess less than five training samples.

Alleviating the data sparseness reasonably may improve the recognition rate remarkably. We further inspect the correlationship between the number of samples and CR. All previously mentioned systems manifest significant correlations at 0.05 level (Rencher 2002) as regards the recognition of Chinese characters. However, their significance is not confirmed with regard to digit and punctuation. This is the main reason that the alleviation of insufficient data by PCA and GVS displays no positive effect. If we expand the available samples of Chinese characters, the performance will be improved further, which can be inferred from Fig. 4.10. As expected, we can see that MQDF3-2 climbs up slower than segmentation-free systems. Data sparseness is a hard problem indeed. However, two principles can alleviate it. The most obvious one is increasing the copies of samples, for example, collecting the same database several times; generating artificial samples by computer [refer to Varga and Bunke (2004) for more details]; incorporating existing character database (we can utilize the isolated-character database to initialize the character models or to produce text lines for a more reliable training); data sharing between similar models. Another principle is to reduce the size of parameter set to be estimated, for example, using dimension reduction method (as in present chapter) or dispensing the number of Gaussians proportional to available samples.

4.7 Conclusions

Realistic Chinese handwriting poses great challenges to the state-of-the-art recognizers. On the one hand, the character separation is still far from solved. The segmentation algorithm falls into under-segmentation, once it encounters touching, overlapping, and crossing phenomena. On the contrary, over-segmentation cases are often raised to left–right structure characters. On the other, due to the great variability in character shape, the character modeling techniques should be updated. Currently, the features are extracted within each character segment. However, the conjunction relationship between adjacent characters also encodes valuable information. Thus, it is in great need to handle these problems.

This chapter describes basic algorithms of HMM-based recognizer for realistic Chinese handwriting under a segmentation-free framework. The text lines fed into recognizer have no need to provide the position of the characters, and the output from recognizer is a best string of characters in MAP sense. Experiments are conducted on HIT-MW database. Promising results are achieved, which not only show the feasibility of the segmentation-free strategy but also provide the apparent evidence on the complementary capacities between the segmentation-free strategy and the segmentation-based one. Based on the observations found in this chapter, we will investigate following points in the next chapter: the enhanced feature extraction method, which can make preferable tradeoff between punctuation and Chinese characters; the synthetic handwriting algorithm to alleviate the insufficient training data; the approach to properly combine segmentation-free and segmentation-based systems, linguistic correction, and discriminative training.

References

Y. Chen, X. Ding, Y. Wu, Off-line handwritten Chinese character recognition based on crossing line feature. In: Proceedings of the fourth international conference on document analysis and recognition, (Ulm, Germany, 1997)

J.E. Freund, *Modern Elementary Statistics* (Prentice-Hall, New Jersey, 1984)

M. Gales, S. Young, The application of hidden Markov models in speech recognition. Found. Trends. Signal Process. **1**(3), 195–304 (2007). doi:10.1561/2000000004

C. Hong, G. Loudon, Y. Wu, R. Zitserman, Segmentation and recognition of continuous handwriting Chinese text. Int. J. Pattern Recognit. Artif. Intell. **12**, 223–232 (1998)

A.L. Koerich, R. Sabourin, C.Y. Suen, Recognition and verification of unconstrained handwritten words. IEEE Trans. Pattern Anal. Mach. Intell. **27**, 1509–1521 (2005)

C.L. Liu, Handwritten Chinese character recognition: effects of shape normalization and feature extraction. In: Arabic and Chinese handwriting recognition (2008)

U.V. Marti, H. Bunke, Using a statistical language model to improve the performance of an HMM-based cursive handwriting recognition system. Int. J. Pattern Recognit. Artif. Intell. **15**, 65–90 (2001)

M. Mohamed, P. Gader, Handwritten word recognition using segmentation free hidden Markov modeling and segmentation-based dynamic programming techniques. IEEE Trans. Pattern Anal. Mach. Intell. **18**, 548–554 (1996)

P. Natarajan, Z. Lu, R.M. Schwartz, I. Bazzi, J. Makhoul, Multilingual machine printed OCR. Int. J. Pattern Recognit. Artif. Intell. **15**, 43–63 (2001)

L.R. Rabiner, A tutorial on Hidden Markov Models and selected applications in speech recognition. Proc. IEEE **77**, 257–285 (1989)

A.C. Rencher, *Methods of Multivariate Analysis* (Wiley, New York, 2002)

T.-H. Su, T.-W. Zhang, D.-J. Guan, Off-line Recognition of Realistic Chinese Handwriting Using Segmentation-free Strategy. Pattern Recognit. **42**(1), 167–182 (2009)

T-H. Su, T-W. Zhang, H-J. Huang, Y. Zhou, HMM-based recognizer with segmentation-free strategy for unconstrained Chinese handwritten text. In: Proceedings of the 9th international conference on document analysis and recognition (2007a)

T-H. Su, T-W. Zhang, Z-W. Qiu, D-J. Guan, Gabor-based recognizer for Chinese handwriting from segmentation-free strategy. In: Proceedings of the 12th international conference on computer analysis of images and patterns (2007b)

T. Varga, H. Bunke, Offline handwriting recognition using synthetic training data produced by means of a geometrical distortion model. Int. J. Pattern Recognit. Artif. Intell. **18**, 1285–1302 (2004)

A. Vinciarelli, S. Bengio, H. Bunke, Offline recognition of unconstrained handwritten texts using HMMs and statistical language models. IEEE Trans. Pattern Anal. Mach. Intell. **26**, 709–720 (2004)

Chapter 5
Segmentation-Free Strategy: Advanced Algorithms

Abstract The hidden Markov model (HMM), a powerful tool, has been widely applied to sequence analysis tasks such as speech recognition and handwriting recognition. However, its recognition performance is normally limited to the general framework. In this chapter, we investigate sophisticated techniques for improving its recognition performance. This includes a method for synthesizing string samples from isolated character images. Second, enhanced features are derived considering the uniqueness of Chinese characters and text line normalization is added to improve feature discrimination. Third, discriminative training based on MPE criteria is explored in the context of Chinese handwriting recognition for the first time. Fourth, a bridge is built between a segmentation-free and a segmentation-based system. This chapter also discusses the distributed training of the bigram language model.

5.1 Introduction

In the previous chapter, HMMs are employed to build a segmentation-free recognizer for Chinese handwriting. Its parameters are learned in a Maximum Likelihood (ML) manner. HMMs scale well to large data set, equipped with efficient learning and inference algorithms like the Baum-Welch algorithm and the Viterbi algorithm. HMM-based handwriting recognition has the merit that the model parameters can be trained with string samples without annotation of character boundaries.

However, the recognition accuracy of segmentation-free system in previous chapter has been limited to a low level. We present sophisticated techniques to improve the recognizer in this chapter. The renewed system architecture is illustrated in Fig. 5.1. During its training stage, all components of the baseline segmentation system are refined (marked with a star).

T. Su, *Chinese Handwriting Recognition: An Algorithmic Perspective*,   99
SpringerBriefs in Electrical and Computer Engineering,
DOI: 10.1007/978-3-642-31812-2_5, © The Author(s) 2013

Fig. 5.1 Renewed system architecture. The renewed components are marked with a star

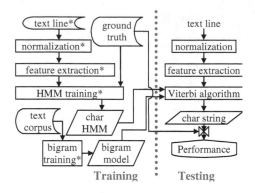

5.2 Ensemble

Considering the output of a recognizer, it can be an item in recognition lexicon or a string of items. Therefore, combining two recognizers results in three types (see Fig. 5.2). The combination of isolated character (type I) is intensively studied and omitted here. We show interest in text line recognition. The research group led by H. Bunke has studied type II with a parallel structure (Marti and Bunke 2001; Bertolami and Bunke 2008). This section presents two ensemble paradigms for Chinese handwriting recognition. Both of them fall into type III.

5.2.1 Curve of Character Matching Rate

Character matching rate (*CMR*) is used to reflect the complementary capacity of two systems at certain recognition rate. Suppose A_i, B_i are the sets of characters whose *CR* is bigger than i % given by two systems, respectively. More specifically, if we assume A_i = {"1", "2", "9", "7"} and B_i = {"2", "9", "7"}, we say $A_i \cap B_i$ (= {"2", "9", "7"}) is the match set between A_i and B_i. The cardinality of the match set is given by $|A_i \cap B_i|$ (= 3, in this example). The *CMR* of them at the *CR* of i % is defined as the normalization of the above cardinality:

$$CMR_i = \frac{|A_i \cap B_i|}{\min\{|A_i|, |B_i|\}}.$$ (5.1)

From the formula, we can see that less matches between two systems, the smaller the value of CMR_i. So, we can use *CMR* to characterize the possible complementary capacities between two systems when *CR* is bigger than i %. The curve of *CMR* manifests the possible complementary capacity dynamically by visualizing the CMR_i vs different i's.

We first plot the *CMR* curve in Fig. 5.3 between 80DFUS and MQDF3-2 (denoted as 80DFUS + MQDF3-2). It can be regarded as the measurement of

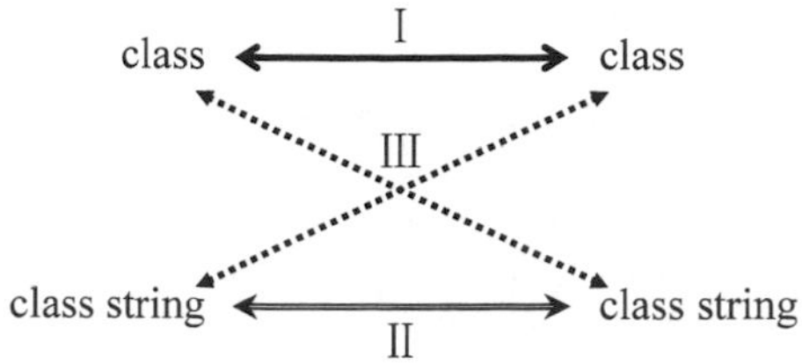

Fig. 5.2 Three types of
ensemble paradigms

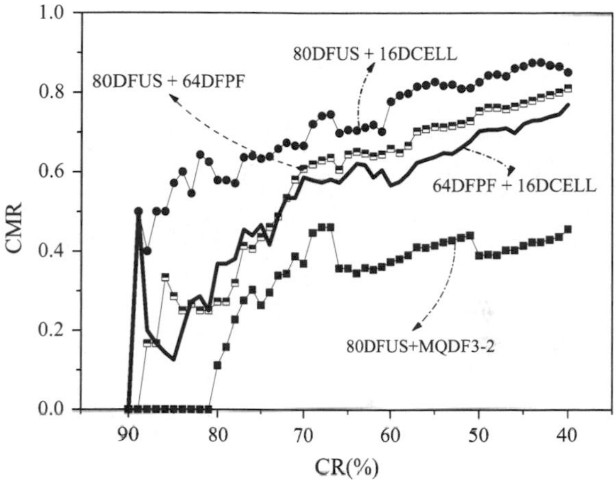

Fig. 5.3 Curves of CMR.
Clear complementary
capacities can be inferred
between the segmentation-
free strategy and the
segmentation-based one.
Reprinted from Ref. (Su et al.
2009), Copyright 2009, with
permission from Elsevier

complementary capacities between two different recognition strategies when they
are trained on the same training data and their features are of the same type.

As references, we add another two *CMR* curves between two different segmentation-free systems: one is 80DFUS and 16DCELL (80DFUS + 16DCELL), the other
is 80DFUS and 64DFPF (80DFUS + 64DFPF). Seen from the previous experiments
in Sect. 4.6.1, the fusion of cell features and FPFs demonstrates apparent improvement to each original set of features. Thus, we also illustrate their *CMR* curve in
Fig. 5.3 (it is labeled as 64DFPF + 16DCELL) to give a more concrete reference.

Seen from the figure, the curve of 80DFUS + MQDF3-2 is completely lower
than other three curves derived from segmentation-free systems. The smallest
differential between them is more than 9 % when *CR* ranges from 40 to 88 %.
Moreover, when more characters are considered (with *CR* decreasing), the differentials may largen. Therefore, we can safely conclude that the two strategies
under same training data may greatly complement each other, even when they
employ the same type of features.

5.2.2 Serial Structure

As the core of the framework, a segmentation-free recognizer is used to locate the
character boundaries bound replacing the character segmentation stage. Its block
diagram is illustrated in Fig. 5.4. First of all, a segmentation-free recognizer based

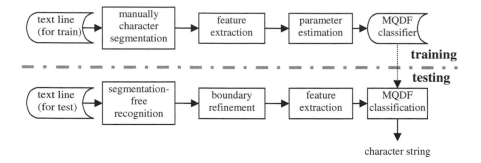

Fig. 5.4 Block diagram of the serial integration of segmentation-free and segmentation-based systems

on enFPF is employed to estimate the rough character boundary. Following that, the boundary is refined further by the projection histogram around the initial boundary. Once a character segment is extracted, the symbol underlying it can be identified by isolated handwritten Chinese character recognition systems.

The output of segmentation-free recognizer not only includes the character string but also the estimated position of each character. However, the positions of characters can only roughly locate the boundary. For better boundary estimation, the position should be tuned by incorporating the characteristics of character boundary. We use an example to show the whole process of projection profile-based refinement.

Supposing the estimated boundary by our recognizer is marked with bold vertical line, we can describe the position with its x_0 coordination as in Fig. 5.5a. We select a neighbor with a radius of R around x and plot its vertical projection profile $\mathbf{h}(x)$ (see Fig. 5.5b). The final boundary x' can be easily obtained which yields minimum of $\mathbf{h}(x)$ (see Fig. 5.5c), that is:

$$x' = \arg \min_{x} \mathbf{h}(x) \ s.t. \ |x - x_0| \le R \tag{5.2}$$

5.2.3 Parallel Structure

A distinct mechanism is presented to provide a concrete evidence for the complementariness between the segmentation-free system (80DFUS) and segmentation-based system (MQDF3-2), as illustrated in Fig. 5.6. A similar strategy for English handwritten word has been presented in Ref. (Mohamed and Gader 1996). If the output of the fed text line is more "confident" than a threshold *TH*, 80DFUS will stand away. Otherwise, we start 80DFUS to give the final output. The confidence is evaluated on the *r*th text line by LL^r as follows:

Fig. 5.5 The process of
boundary refinement. **a** Initial
boundary before the
refinement. **b** Vertical
projection profile around the
initial boundary. **c** Final
boundary after the refinement

(a)

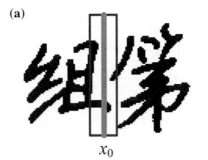

x_0

(b)

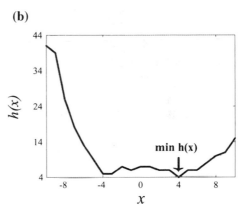

(c)

x'

$$LL^r = M^r_{cs} - M^r_{df} \qquad (5.3)$$

where M^r_{cs} measures the quality of character segmentation and M^r_{df} measures the
closeness of discriminant function.

Initially, M^r_{cs} and M^r_{df} are zeros. If the width of any character segments are
larger than 1.5 times average character width (58 pixels in our experiment), M^r_{cs}
will be updated with $M^r_{cs} \leftarrow M^r_{cs} + 1$. To diminish the effect of text line length, M^r_{cs}
will be divided by the number of average characters in the rth text line. Similarly,
M^r_{df} increases with 10, if any of the differentials of minimum two $g_3(x, \omega_i)$ is

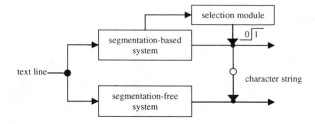

Fig. 5.6 Block diagram of the parallel integration of segmentation-free and segmentation-based systems. Segmentation-free system can be started simultaneously with segmentation-based system. Gating modular determines whose result is delivered of two member systems to each text line

smaller than 0.34. Also, the M_{df}^{r} should be divided by the number of character segments in the rth text line.

5.3 Feature Enhancement

An enhanced four plane feature (enFPF) is first provided. Then Delta information is further utilized to encode contextual dependency.

5.3.1 Enhanced FPF (enFPF)

FPF is originally used in the isolated handwritten Chinese character recognition (Chen et al. 1997). It generates directional planes using stroke run-length analysis and unfortunately, small strokes (especially to punctuation marks and digits) and salient pixels on the flange of strokes are sometimes discarded. We enhance the planes by integrating most of the above strokes and pixels. Supposing the foreground pixel is "1" and background one "0", the process works as follows:

Step 1. Generate the initial directional planes. Each text line image (it is denoted as OT) is scanned in four directions (horizontal, vertical, right diagonal, and left diagonal) and only the strokes are retained which are longer than a threshold $c \times SW$ (SW denotes the average stroke width and c is a constant). SW is estimated on the whole text line by an analysis of stroke histogram (as in Sect. 2.4.4). The four planes are marked as HT, VT, RT, and LT, respectively. Currently, the parameter c is set to 1.5.

Step 2. Enhance above planes. Planes in Step 1 comprise line elements. Compared with the actual strokes, certain portion may be unreasonably discarded, especially in the stroke ends. Such finding motivates us to add the discarded portions upon the initial planes:

(a)

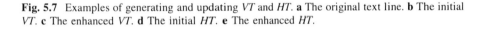

(b)

(c)

(d)

(e)

Fig. 5.7 Examples of generating and updating *VT* and *HT*. **a** The original text line. **b** The initial *VT*. **c** The enhanced *VT*. **d** The initial *HT*. **e** The enhanced *HT*.

$$VT \leftarrow VT \cup (OT \cap \sim(HT \cup RT \cup LT)), \tag{5.4}$$

where $\cup$, $\cap$, and $\sim$ are logic AND, OR and NOT operators, respectively. The planes in the right side are the initial directional planes. *HT*, *RT* and *LT* can be updated similarly. The evolution of *VT* and *HT* is exemplified in Fig. 5.7 (added pixels are rendered with blue color). Obviously, the following equation is true:

$$HT \cup VT \cup RT \cup LT = OT. \tag{5.5}$$

This means that the original image can be completely reconstructed by the four planes.

Step 3. Partition sliding window at each plane into smaller cells. Currently, 8 × 2 uniform cells are drawn per window.

Step 4. Extract directional features. To each plane, the scanning lines are perpendicular to the stroke direction. For instance, as regards the vertical plane, the scanning line runs horizontally. Previously, the stroke count in each cell is increased by one every transition from foreground to background. Herein, both transient from foreground and that into foreground can invoke the addition. Eventually, all counts (8 × 2 × 4) in current window are concatenated together as the feature vector.

5.3.2 Delta Features

Delta features are equipped in most speech recognition systems for their ability to grasp the temporal dependence (Gales and Young 2007). The Delta features are the first order linear regression coefficients derived from static features (Furui 1986):

$$
\Delta \mathbf{o}_t = \frac{\sum_{i=-n}^{n} i \cdot \mathbf{o}_{t+i}}{\sum_{i=-n}^{n} i^2}
$$
$$
= \frac{\sum_{i=1}^{n} i \cdot (\mathbf{o}_{t+i} - \mathbf{o}_{t-i})}{2 \sum_{i=1}^{n} i^2},
$$

(5.6)

where $\mathbf{o}_t$ is the vector of static features. The Delta feature involves $2n + 1$ windows for regression. In handwritten images, it reflects the slope in each feature dimension. The derivative features used in (Natarajan et al. 2008; Ge and Huo 2002) can be viewed as special cases of Eq. (5.3). Delta features are dynamically derived and can express the dependence among consecutive observations. This compensates HMMs for the loss resulting from the conditional independence assumption.

5.4 Text Line Normalization

Text line normalization is a significant step to reduce the variability of different writing style. To increase the robustness of the segmentation-free baseline, we employ three techniques to renew the above baseline recognizer. First, variance truncation (VT) is used to regulate the Gaussian mixture density: the variance of each dimension is truncated to the average variance if it is smaller than this value. Second, the Box-Cox transformation (BCT) is applied to enFPF features to make the values more Gaussian-like and thus benefits recognition. We empirically selected a power of 0.4 in BCT. In addition, we normalize the height of each text line to reduce the within-class variability of character samples. The height of a text line is estimated from connected components by bounding consecutive M blocks and averaging the height of the bounding boxes (Liu et al. 2002). The text line image is rescaled to a standard height, *stdH*.

5.5 Synthesizing Samples

Considering the large number of Chinese character categories and the severe sparseness of handwritten string image data, we synthesize string images from existing isolated character samples for HMM training. Synthesizing string samples has been practiced in English word recognition. In (Varga 2006), training samples were expanded by distorting realistic text lines. In (Thomas et al. 2009), individual

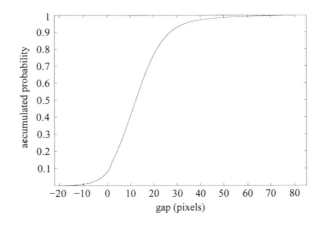

Fig. 5.8 Accumulative gap histogram. © [2010] IEEE. Reprinted, with permission, from Ref. (Su and Liu 2010)

characters are concatenated using a ligature joining algorithm for natural-shape handwriting. We investigate the techniques for synthesizing Chinese string samples from isolated character samples and our emphasis is how to effectively utilize these samples rather than generate linguistically natural handwriting. In light of above principle, we approximate the distribution of between-character gaps and draw character samples without replacement. By combining Delta features and training with synthetic string samples, we have achieved a large improvement of recognition accuracy in Chinese handwriting recognition.

There have been large databases of isolated Chinese character samples for training classifiers but the number of text line images is very small. Isolated character samples can be directly used to train character HMMs but the collocation between characters cannot be modeled by training with isolated characters. To alleviate the sparseness of text line data, we synthesize string image samples from isolated character images.

String samples are generated through concatenating existing isolated character samples of the same image resolution. If we have already picked K character samples up, then the task is to concatenate them into a string image whose purpose is to effectively utilize isolated character samples. To synthesize a text line, thus the following problems should be solved: how to draw a character class, how to select a sample for a certain class, how to join a sequence of character samples together. Since the samples in each class often are assumed of equal importance, we draw samples uniformly providing that the character class is known.

Character samples are concatenated together through between-character gaps. Gap between two samples are randomly generated from a gap histogram. To approximate the gaps, we first mark each left and right boundaries of characters in the training text lines. Then the difference between the left position of current character and the right position of previous one is collected to derive a gap histogram. If character overlapping occurs, the gap may be negative. The accumulative gap histogram is illustrated in Fig. 5.8. The binary search is used to locate the gap corresponding to a random number.

Algorithm 5.1 gives the skeleton to produce a text line. Step 2~6 recursively draw samples. All selected class names and samples in current text line are temporarily recorded. Steps 4 and 5 express a stratified sampling paradigm. We can first draw a class from a lexicon, and then we dispatch a sample instance to the class. Each class may associate a weight, indicating its probability to be sampled in Step 4. We may consider uniform (zero-gram), unigram, and bigram statistics in Sect. 5.8.6 respectively. Steps 7 and 8 normalize current text line to a standard height. Step 9 concatenates a sample sequence together with random gaps. The x_{kj}s are aligned in vertical middle line. The last two steps produce feature observations and corresponding ground truth. Algorithm 5.1 can be called as many times as desired or till there leaves no available isolated character samples.

Algorithm 5.1 Synthesizing a text line from isolated character samples
Input:
      $\{(L_i, X_i)\}$: character samples;
      H_c: distribution of the length of strings;
      H_g: distribution of the gaps;
      $stdH$: standard height;
      K: the number of characters in this line;
Output:
      f: features matrix of the string sample;
      l: ground truth of the string sample;
1    $k \leftarrow 0$;
2   **while** $(k \leqslant K)$ **do**
3          $k \leftarrow k+1$;
4   Draw a character class L_k and save it;
5   Draw a sample $x_{kj} (\in X_k)$ and save it;
6   **end while**
7   Estimate height of the textline $estH$ based on the maximum height of each consecutive K samples;
8   Scale each x_{kj} with a factor of $stdH/estH$;
9   Generate $K-1$ gaps and through which x_{kj}s are linked together;
10   Concatenate L_ks as l;
11   Extract enFPF and Delta features, f.

Also, sampling can be done with replacement or without replacement. In our system, isolated character samples are drawn without replacement. This kind of sampling deliberately avoids choosing any sample more than once. If all samples of a character class are exhausted, the class will never be picked up again in the following steps. It stops when samples of all classes are exhausted. Unlikely, random sampling can be done with replacement, however, even in a Bootstrap manner, only 63.21 % of samples can be picked up.

5.6 Distributed N-gram Training

The MapReduce programming model (Dean and Ghemawat 2004) is suitable for large data in a large number of parallel computing nodes. A map function accepts a pair of input (key, value), and generates a pair of output, and then by the reduce function to merge these data with the same key to get the final results. The whole basic process is showed in Fig. 5.9.

MapReduce first get pieces of data (for the user may be a mini-batch training samples), read from multiple nodes to split the data into the (key, value) in the form of input. After processing, It generate the same output format, after shuffling and sorting, the reducer finishes data aggregation and write the output file.

Hadoop is an open-source distributed platform built on HDFS (Hadoop Distributed Filesystem). It also implements MapReduce framework, and provides users with data-intensive distributed applications, whose low layer is transparent. A multinode Hadoop cluster includes a host and multiple nodes. The master node includes one JobTracker, TaskTracker, NameNode, and Datanodes. Worker node

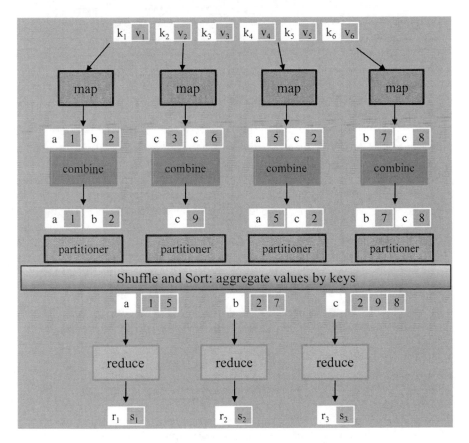

Fig. 5.9 MapReduce working flow chart

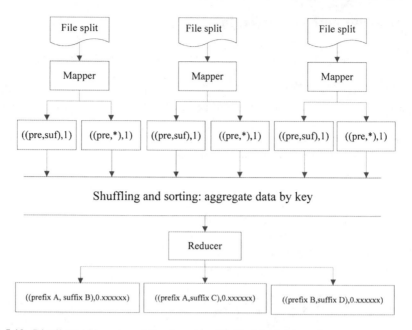

Fig. 5.10 Distributed bigram modeling based on MapReduce framework

includes a DataNode and TaskTracker. Although single data nodes or single cal-
culation nodes can exist, these are usually only used for nonstandard applications.
Hadoop needs the support of JRE 1.6 or later version. The standard startup and
shutdown scripts need to be established between the nodes of the cluster using SSH.

Distributed bigram modeling process is shown in Fig. 5.10.

The bigram modeling is divided into two functions: Mapper and Reducer.
Mapper read into every word, and gives two outputs, one output (prefix, suffix, 1),
indicating that the phrase appears once; another output ([prefix,*], 1), indicating
that the word is the prefix phrase.

The Reducer generated key pairs: count the number of occurrences of (A,B) in
the entire article, and then divided by the number of (A,*) appears (* indicates an
arbitrary suffix): for a specific (A, B) so can calculate (A, B) probability of
occurrence (such as A can refer to 我, and B refers to 们, * includes 们, 爱, 军,
国… etc.). To avoid incomplete statistics of the previous steps, we just employ one
instance of Reducer. In principle, multiple instances of Reducer can also be used.

5.7 MPE/MWE Training

The previous chapter has described how maximum likelihood (ML)-based estimates of the HMM model parameters can be initialized and estimated. In ML
training, only the samples belonging to the class are used to train the

corresponding model. By contrast, the discriminative training approach takes into account all samples of competitive classes. Discriminative training has demonstrated an improvement in recognition accuracy over ML training in many HMM-based speech recognition applications (Jiang 2010). However, the applications of discriminative training in HMMs for Chinese handwriting recognition are scant. This subsection introduces MPE/MWE criterion which is a popular discriminative training objective function in speech recognition. Compared to MMI and MCE criteria, MPE/MWE is aimed for performance optimization at substring level and it has been argued that MPE/MWE is a more appropriate criterion to optimize than the MMI and MCE criteria (Povey 2004).

Supposing S^r denotes the ground truth of the rth text line, the MPE criterion aims to minimize the following objective function (Gales and Young 2007):

$$L_{\mathrm{MPE}}(\lambda) = \sum_{r=1}^{R} \frac{\sum_{S} p_\lambda(\mathbf{O}^r|S)^\kappa P(S) \mathrm{E}(S, S^r)}{\sum_{S} p_\lambda(\mathbf{O}^r|S)^\kappa P(S)} \tag{5.7}$$

where the parameter κ is used to rescale the large range of HMM likelihoods. The error function $\mathrm{E}(S, S^r)$ measures the loss in the substring level like, for example, the approximate phone error (Povey 2004). Here, the summation is over all possible character sequences (falls into MWE). In practice this is restricted to the set of confusable hypotheses. MPE/MWE criterion can be optimized through the extended Baum-Welch (EBW) algorithm.

5.8 Experiments

The sophisticated algorithms are used to improve the performance of segmentation-free recognizer and evluations on them are provided in this section. All except MPE training are tested on HIT-MW database. Considering the high training cost, the advantage of MPE training is demonstrated on a lightweight database, HIT-SW database.

5.8.1 HIT-SW Database

A lightweight database named HIT-SW (HIT is the abbr. of Harbin Institute of Technology, and SW means it is produced by a single writer) is used to evaluate the MPE training in Sect. 5.8.7. All the processes are the same as the collection of HIT-MW database with the exception of the number of writers. Totally there are 83 handwritten documents capturing some important aspects of real handwriting, such as miswriting, erasure, character touching, document skewness, et al.

After text line extraction, all of 798 handwritten lines are successfully separated. We randomly draw 200 of them as test set (4926 characters), 500 as train set (12670 characters), and the remainders (including 98 lines) as validation set (1470 characters). The validation set here is used to tune the parameters, such as the number of Gaussian components in mixture density and training iterations, which will be used to evaluate the recognizer's performance on test set.

As mentioned previously, an HMM is produced per character. In addition, the erasure is also modeled as an HMM. Eventually, there are 1,695 character models.

5.8.2 Evaluation of enFPF

The recognition rates of FPF and enFPF are summarized as the first two rows in Table 5.1. The higher rates under each character type are highlighted with bold font. Since there are merely 8 instances of English letters in test set, their results are not considered.

It can be seen that the enhancement of directional plane averagely increase the CR and AR with 1.80 percent and 0.77 percent, respectively. Among digits, punctuation marks and Chinese characters, the performance of punctuation marks is the most beneficial one. More than 10 percent of improvement in CR and AR is obtained. Another noticeable improvement lies in the CR of digit. The reason underlying above superiority is that the Step 3 of enFPF integrates the small strokes of punctuation mark and digit which are often discarded by FPF (as in Step 2). The smallest improvement to FPF is found in AR of Chinese character. To explore its confidence, we first calculate the AR of each text line by FPF and enFPF, respectively. As a result, 383 pairs of ARs are obtained. Then we can conduct Wilcoxon signed-rank test (Freund 1984). Using above method, their statistical significance holds at 0.0001 level.

We also investigate the performance of Gabor feature and Gradient feature. These two features are preferred in the isolated handwritten Chinese character recognition. In (Su et al. 2007), Gabor feature is successfully adapted into segmentation-free framework and best recognition rates (both CR and AR) are achieved among three examined features when tested on 200 handwritten text lines produced by a single writer. If we perform Sobel operator on a whole text line

Table 5.1 The comparisons of recognition rates among several systems (%)

	Digit		Punctuation		Chinese character		Average	
	CR	AR	CR	AR	CR	AR	CR	AR
FPF	42.17	37.83	32.32	28.66	35.97	**32.98**	35.79	32.71
en-FPF	**55.65**	**45.65**	**44.19**	**39.77**	**36.33**	32.43	**37.59**	**33.48**
Gradient	38.26	29.13	39.39	27.40	33.80	29.52	34.45	29.31
Gabor	27.39	25.65	31.19	24.87	33.87	29.40	33.44	28.87

© [2008] IEEE. Reprinted with modification, with permission, from Ref. (Su et al. 2008)

Table 5.2 The recognition rates of integrated system on test set

	Average (%)	
	CR	AR
MQDF3-2	35.49	33.03
80DFUS	36.38	31.85
Parallel ensemble	40.41	35.69

instead of a character, the Gradient feature (Cheriet et al. 2007) can also be used in segmentation-free framework. We first decompose the gradient vectors into 8 standard directions. Next, we merge each pair of directional planes of opposite directions into orientation plane to give an identical length of feature vector. In addition, an 11 by 11 Gaussian filter (with the standard deviation of 3.6) is used to reduce its dependence on the stroke position.

The results of Gabor feature and Gradient feature are also shown in Table 5.1 (the last two rows). However, their performance is inferior to both FPF and en-FPF. As for Gradient feature, our experiments on the isolated handwritten Chinese character recognition have show that it is much dependent on the shape normalization process. Unfortunately, no shape normalization has been applied in segmentation-free framework yet. As for Gabor feature, it is more sensitive to the variety in stroke width. In multiple-writer handwriting, stroke widths are frequently varied though uniformly distributed in single-writer case.

The number of training samples has a significant effect on the final recognition rates. We plot the average CRs of Chinese characters using above features versus the sample size of the character class in Fig. 5.11. It is obvious that enFPF is superior to others.

Fig. 5.11 Relationship between the number of samples and CR. © [2008] IEEE. Reprinted, with permission, from Ref. (Su et al. 2008)

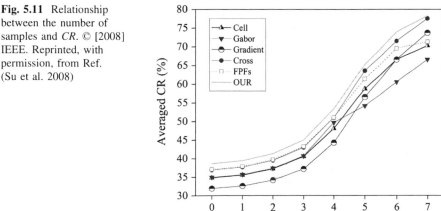

5.8.3 Evaluation of Ensemble Classifiers

5.8.3.1 Parallel ensemble

The parallel integrated system in Fig. 5.6 works well, and the results when $TH = 111$ pixels are shown in Table 5.2. The base segmentation-free system is 80DFUS (Cf. Chap. 4); the base segmentation-based system is MQDF3-2 (Cf. Sect. 3.8.3.1). We can see an obvious improvement in average recognition rates. It consumes 3078.01 ms on the desktop PC and 1002.38 ms on the laptop (the description of computers is listed in Table 4.4).

5.8.3.2 Serial Ensemble

Generally, better the quality of the character segmentation, better the recognition results. The segmentation-free recognizer is used to estimate the initial character boundaries. The boundaries are further tuned to improve the quality of the character segmentation. These efforts are expected to extract a better segmentation result than classical algorithms.

This subsection evaluates and compares the character segmentation rates of ensemble methods, Hong algorithm and Liu algorithm. The segmentation-free system presented in Sect. 5.8.2 is selected to provide initial character boundaries. The *SCR* results on digit, punctuation, and Chinese character are separately calculated and given in Table 5.3.

We first compare the second and the fourth rows. On average, our method has increased the *SCR* by 17.51 % than Hong algorithm. Among digit, punctuation, and Chinese character, the former two types are two most beneficial ones. More than 20 % of improvement is obtained to them. Hong algorithm has supposed that characters are uniformly distributed in size. However, in the realistic Chinese handwriting, above statement seldom holds yet. The overwhelming difference among digit, punctuation, and Chinese character in their size results in relatively low *SCR*.

Then we compare the third and fourth rows. Consistent advantages are also observed on all character types in our method even when boundaries are not refined. The smallest improvement is larger than 1%.

By comparing the last two rows, we can see a significant role of the boundary refinement. The average *SCR* achieves 8.08 % of improvement. The minimal and

Table 5.3 Comparison of *SCR* (%)

	Digit	Punctuation	Chinese character	Average
Hong algorithm	16.96	21.59	65.67	60.26
Liu algorithm	40.00	44.44	74.23	70.51
Ensemble (w/o refinement)	44.35	45.45	75.41	71.77
Ensemble (w/ refinement)	47.83	60.35	82.87	79.81

Table 5.4 Comparison of SPR and SBR

	SPR	*SBR*
Hong algorithm	71.27	−15.45
Liu algorithm	63.13	10.89
Ensemble (w/o refinement)	73.62	−2.52
Ensemble (w/refinement)	82.26	−3.00

maximal improvements among digit, punctuation, and Chinese character are 3.48 and 14.90 %, respectively.

Further, we collect the *SPR* and *SBR* of ensemble methods, besides the Hong algorithm and Liu algorithm and illustrate them in Table 5.4. When there is no boundary refinement, the *SPR* of ensemble method can achieve 2.35 and 10.49 % of improvement than Hong algorithm and Liu algorithm, respectively. The boundary refinement increases the SPR with extra 8.64 %.

The sign of the *SBR* can mostly reflect the tendency in under-segmentation and over-segmentation and its absolute value encodes the degree of the tendency. It seems that the segmentation results of Hong algorithm demonstrate severe under-segmentation and opposite effect is observed in Liu algorithm. Compared with them, ensemble methods only present a slight under-segmentation.

Two segmentation examples by these methods are illustrated respectively in Figs. 5.12 and 5.13. The character path by ensemble methods is denoted as single vertical line, while Hong algorithm marks the left and right boundaries and Liu algorithm uses boxes.

Ensemble methods have been justified when inspected in character segmentation stage. However, the evidence is not yet sufficient . The final recognition

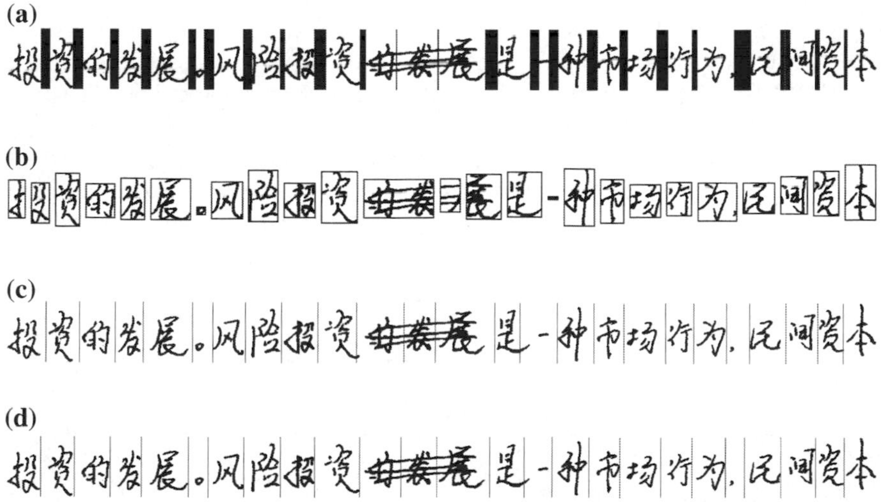

Fig. 5.12 Segmentation examples by four algorithms. **a** Hong algorithm (segments are detached with equidistance). **b** Liu algorithm. **c** Ensemble method without boundary refinement. **d** Ensemble algorithm with boundary refinement

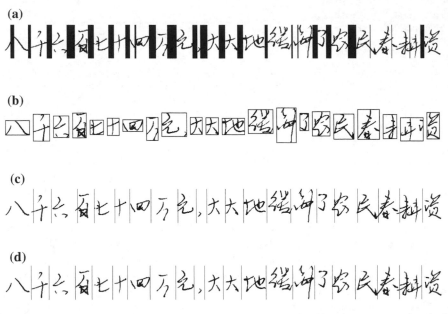

Fig. 5.13 Segmentation examples by four algorithms **a** Hong algorithm (segments are detached with equidistance). **b** Liu algorithm. **c** Ensemble method without boundary refinement. **d** Ensemble algorithm with boundary refinement

performance may present inconsistence with that of the character segmentation, since character segmentation stage is just a component of a whole system. Thus, we evaluate their recognition performance.

In the following, we will first show the advantages of ensemble methods than Hong-based and Liu-based ones. Four classifiers seen previously as MQDF3-3–MQDF3-6 in Chap. 3 are used to identify each character segment. Table 5.5 summarizes the recognition results of MQDF3-3 and MQDF3-4. The average *CR* and *AR* of ensemble recognizer are 12.12 and 10.36 % higher than those of Hong-based recognizer. The advantages are revealed on all character types and especially the relative improvement in *CR* or *AR* ranges from 153 to 202 % to the digit and punctuation, respectively.

Table 5.5 The recognition results of combined systems with serial structure, system based on Hong algorithm and system based on Liu algorithm where MQDF3-3/MQDF3-4 are used

Systems	DI (%)		PU (%)		CH (%)		Avg (%)	
	CR	*AR*	*CR*	*AR*	*CR*	*AR*	*CR*	*AR*
MQDF3-3	18.70	12.61	16.79	14.14	44.53	42.09	41.23	38.67
MQDF3-4	37.83	−5.22	39.14	18.06	50.69	37.66	49.25	34.65
Ensemble (MQDF3-3, w/o refinement)	43.91	32.61	31.19	22.22	51.32	47.31	49.23	44.55
Ensemble (MQDF3-3, w/ refinement)	47.39	36.09	50.25	42.68	53.87	50.11	53.35	49.03

Table 5.6 The recognition results of combined systems with serial structure, system based on Hong algorithm and system based on Liu algorithm where MQDF3-5/MQDF3-6 are used

Systems	DI (%)		PU (%)		CH (%)		Avg (%)	
	CR	AR	CR	AR	CR	AR	CR	AR
MQDF3-5	19.13	13.48	14.39	9.85	49.27	47.20	45.18	42.78
MQDF3-6	37.39	−19.13	31.57	6.94	54.06	41.77	51.49	36.84
Ensemble (MQDF3-5, w/o refinement)	47.39	29.13	27.78	14.27	55.00	48.68	52.24	44.92
Ensemble (MQDF3-5, w/ refinement)	49.57	39.13	42.55	32.70	58.84	55.39	57.06	52.82

Consistent advantages are observed on all character types in our recognizer, comparing with the recognizer based on Liu algorithm. The average *CR* and *AR* of ours are increased by 4.10 and 14.38 %, respectively. To digit and punctuation, there are more remarkable improvements in *CR* and *AR*, which range from 9.56 to 41.31 %. Noticeable differentials in the *CR* and *AR* of Liu-based recognizer are detected. Connected component analysis employed by Liu algorithm may tend to split multistructure Chinese characters and results in a large insertion error in the recognition results.

The boundary refinement can be justified, comparing the last two rows of Table 5.5. On averagely, there are 4.12 and 4.48 % of improvements in *CR* and *AR*, respectively. Further inspection shows that the improvement on punctuation is the most obvious one, which accounts for about 20 % of improvement in both *CR* and *AR*.

Finally, we list the results when replacing MQDF3-3 and MQDF3-4 with MQDF3-5 and MQDF3-6 in Table 5.6. Similar advantages of ensemble methods can be observed.

5.8.4 Evaluation of Text Line Normalization

Techniques including text line normalization used to renew the baseline are evaluated and their results are shown in Table 5.7. Seen from the table, VT increases the *CR/AR* by 8–10 %, BCT receives 1.1–1.7 % improvements, and HN ($M = 6$, $stdH = 80$ pixels) improve the rates with about 1 % in addition. Renewed baseline yields at least 11 % improvements than previous results totally.

Table 5.7 Construct renewed baseline incrementally (%)

Methods	Digit		Punctuation		Chinese character		Average	
	CR	AR	CR	AR	CR	AR	CR	AR
enFPF	55.65	45.65	**44.19**	**39.77**	36.33	32.43	37.59	33.48
VT	52.17	45.65	6.69	5.18	49.98	**46.80**	45.95	42.83
BCT	62.61	52.17	21.47	18.43	49.99	46.51	47.62	44.00
HN (Renewed baseline)	**67.83**	**53.48**	27.53	25.25	**50.73**	46.62	**48.98**	**44.77**

Variance truncation (VT), Box-Cox transformation (BCT), and height normalization (HN) are applied on the previous system. © [2010] IEEE. Reprinted, with permission, from Ref. (Su and Liu 2010)

Table 5.8 Evaluation of Delta features (%)

Methods	Digit		Punctuation		Chinese character		Average	
	CR	*AR*	*CR*	*AR*	*CR*	*AR*	*CR*	*AR*
HN (Renewed baseline)	**67.83**	**53.48**	27.53	25.25	50.73	46.62	48.98	44.77
Adding Delta features	59.13	38.26	**43.18**	**40.40**	**52.90**	**48.70**	**52.11**	**47.60**

5.8.5 Evaluation of Delta Features

We merely append (first order) Delta features for the demonstration purpose. The static features are enFPF. The parameter n in Eq. (5.6) is set as 8 through validation. The results are listed in Table 5.8. Compared with the baseline, about 3 % improvement is observed. We further investigate the effect of Delta features for Chinese characters and plot the *CR* as regard to sample size in Fig. 5.14. From the figure, we can see that Delta features facilitate classes of large samples, without loss in those of small samples. In addition, Delta features (first two orders) demonstrate strengths than derivative features that are presented in (Ge and Huo 2002; Natarajan et al. 2008) when dimensionality reduction is carried out.

5.8.6 Evaluation of Synthetic Samples

We evaluate the efficacy of synthetic string samples through recognition results. Before retraining the HMMs three passes, we append the synthetic string samples and reduce the variance threshold to truncate each Gaussian component by half. The recognition results are given in Tables 5.9, 5.10, and Fig. 5.15; a recognition example is demonstrated in Fig. 5.16. First, the effect of a bigram language model is considered. The bigram statistics are derived from People's Daily corpus with 79,509,778 characters. Second, the sampling methods, with replacement and without replacement are evaluated separately. The sampling with replacement draws the same number of character samples as without replacement. Third, the process of drawing samples is guided by three kinds of linguistic contexts. More strong the linguistic contexts, more linguistically natural the synthetic text line looks. In addition, the results produced by character training are also provided.

From Tables 5.9, 5.10, and Fig. 5.15, we simply highlight the following three points. First, the sampling without replacement performs better. During sampling with replacement, if the underlying text is generated by bigram statistics, the synthetic image looks linguistically natural. However, the parameters of HMMs can hardly be robustly learned, since samples of some classes may be chosen multiple times, while portions of samples never be accessed (Cf. Fig. 5.15a and b).

Second, using synthetic text lines has clear advantages than character training to learn HMM parameters when recognition couples a bigram language model.

Fig. 5.14 Evaluation of
Delta features concerning
Chinese character (*CR* vs
sample size of the character
class)

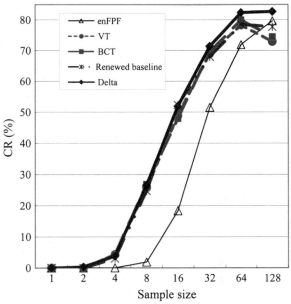

The most fundamental distinction between text line training and character training
is that the adjacent characters in a text line compete with each other for parameter
estimation of their classes. Such competitions benefit postprocessing with a bigram
language model.

Third, as for without replacement strategy, the uniform, unigram and bigram-
guided sampling techniques perform comparably well. Though sampling can be
guided by linguistic statistics, the underlying text of the synthetic images is biased
much toward the uniform distribution, since the same sets of isolated characters are
used. Further inspection (Cf. Fig. 5.15c and d) shows that uniform-guided technique
performs slight better if bigram language model is equipped with recognition, while
unigram and bigram-guided techniques are slight better when recognition without
bigram language model. As for uniform-guided technique, a character class can
follow any character classes, thus each character HMM has the equal chance to
compete with each other. Unlikely, the character classes of high frequency are
picked up with large chances using unigram or bigram-guided technique and their
samples are exhausted in earlier stage. As a consequence, the competitions between
the classes of high frequency and those of low frequency are much limited.

How about fixed between-character gaps instead of histogram-based one? We
evaluate two kinds of fixed gaps: 1 pixel and one-fifth of *stdH* (16 pixels). Character
sampling is done uniformly without replacement. The average recognition rates are
70.77 %/65.22 %, 73.01 %/69.51 % (*CR/AR*) respectively. Histogram gap yields at
least 0.88 % improvement. From Fig. 5.15c and d, synthesizing string samples using
fixed gaps shares some properties with character training.

There exists a few related works in offline recognition of Chinese handwriting.
Actually, they are not comparable, since they are not trained on the same data or

Table 5.9 Evaluation of synthesized methods (%)

Draw Methods	Digit		Punctuation		Chinese character		Average	
	CR	AR	CR	AR	CR	AR	CR	AR
Uniform & with rep	59.13	50.00	41.92	39.27	61.51	58.43	59.55	56.36
Unigram & with rep	60.00	47.83	43.56	40.15	61.29	57.92	59.54	55.93
Bigram & with rep	58.26	50.43	37.50	35.86	61.16	58.58	58.81	56.18
Uniform & without rep	55.22	46.09	43.56	41.54	63.97	60.85	61.76	58.59
Unigram & without rep	55.65	48.26	42.05	40.53	64.29	61.49	61.91	59.12
Bigram & without rep	59.13	48.70	44.82	41.79	64.45	61.28	62.41	59.06
Char training	62.17	47.39	47.85	41.41	63.54	60.38	61.97	58.20

Language model is not used. © [2010] IEEE. Reprinted, with permission, from Ref. (Su and Liu 2010)

Table 5.10 Evaluation of synthesized methods (%)

Draw Methods	Digit		Punctuation		Chinese character		Average	
	CR	AR	CR	AR	CR	AR	CR	AR
Uniform & with rep	70.44	65.22	59.97	49.49	72.31	69.62	71.04	67.56
Unigram & with rep	72.61	69.13	57.95	48.48	72.73	70.29	71.27	68.16
Bigram & with rep	70.00	67.39	57.20	49.24	72.90	70.42	71.29	68.29
Uniform & without rep	70.87	65.65	60.48	51.26	75.04	72.46	73.49	70.22
Unigram & without rep	69.57	65.22	59.85	50.51	75.60	73.33	73.89	70.91
Bigram & without rep	70.43	64.35	60.98	51.77	75.24	72.91	73.7	70.64
Char training	70.43	64.35	62.37	41.29	68.8	65.93	68.18	63.52

Bigram language model is coupled. © [2010] IEEE. Reprinted, with permission, from Ref. (Su and Liu 2010)

they are developed from different motivations, and even they are tested on different test sets. As possible references to readers, we list them below. In (Natarajan et al. 2008), BBN recognition system is presented based on HMMs, where the best *AR* metric is less than 38 % on their in-house Chinese handwriting databases. In (Wang et al. 2009), segmentation recognition-integrated strategy is presented. It recognizes 58 % of the characters without language models, and the best recognition rate is about 78 % after incorporating the scores from a restricted Gaussian classifier and language models.

5.8.7 Evaluation of MPE/MWE Training

To each training textline, multiple alternative transcriptions are generated. We select the 10 most confusable ones which are used to compute the denominator in Eq. (5.7). In the training stage, just mean vector of each Gaussian is adjusted.

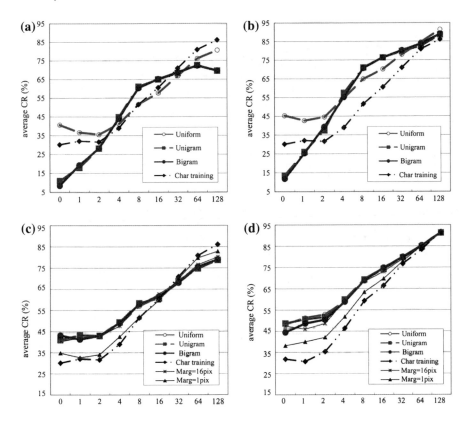

Fig. 5.15 Chinese character *CR* over different sample sizes. **a** sample drawing with replacement and recognition without bigram; **b** sample drawing with replacement and recognition with bigram; **c** sample drawing without replacement and recognition without bigram, **d** sample drawing without replacement and recognition with bigram. © [2010] IEEE. Reprinted, with permission, from Ref. (Su and Liu 2010)

During the decoding stage, a weak bigram language is incorporated which is derived from the small text corpus of training data. Due to the heavy training cost, we merely experiment on HIT-SW database.

As a baseline writer-dependent recognizer, enFPF and the Delta features are employed. For a robust training, 50 copies of distorted textline (Cf. (Varga 2006) for the distortion method) are added into training set. The complete results are given in Table 5.11. From the table, MPE/MWE training improves the recognition rates more than one percent. By the way, it also suggests that the sophisticated algorithms (such as enhanced features, synthesizing samples, language correction) used to boost the writer-independent recognition systems are applicable to writer-dependent recognizer.

(a)

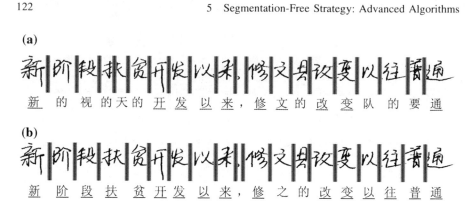

(b)

Fig. 5.16 Recognition results coupling a bigram.The correct outputs are underlined. © [2010] IEEE. Reprinted, with permission, from Ref. (Su and Liu 2010) (**a**) using isolated character training (**b**) using synthetic text line training (uniform sampling, without replacement)

Table 5.11 Evaluation of MPE/MWE training on HIT-SW database	Methods	Average (%)	
		CR	*AR*
	enFPF	80.35	76.93
	Adding Delta features	83.01	81.41
	Adding Synthetic samples	84.93	83.11
	MPE training	86.38	84.15
	Bigram	89.39	87.65

5.8.8 Evaluation of Distributed N-gram Training

For People's Daily corpus with 79509778 Chinese characters, the CPU time used to derive a bigram is compared between standalone mode and distributed mode. The standalone program consumes about 4 minutes and 45 seconds to generate a bigram without smoothing. The speed of the distributed program depends on its number of nodes. In the case of four nodes, the speed is about 2 minutes and 29 seconds to generate the same model, as shown in Fig. 5.17. The results manifest desirable CPU time savage.

5.9 Conclusions

Several sophisticated algorithms are covered to improve the performance of segmentation-free systems. These techniques include: (1) two ensemble paradigms between segmentation-free system and a segmentation-based system; (2) enFPF and Delta features; (3) synthesize string samples from isolated character images; (4) textline normalization; (5) linguistic context estimation and utilization; (6)

Fig. 5.17 Distributed bigram modeling: efficiency versus the number of nodes

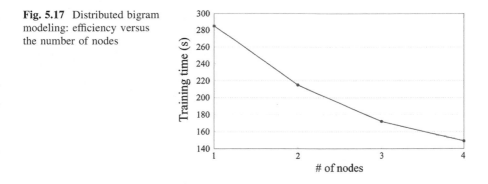

MPE/MWE training. All of them are tested on standard database and their advantages are observed. Properly combining them can make a steady progress for a practical Chinese handwriting recognizer.

References

R. Bertolami, H. Bunke, Hidden Markov Model-based ensemble methods for offline handwritten text line recognition. Pattern Recogn. **41**(11), 3346–3452 (2008)

Y. Chen, X. Ding, Y. Wu, Off-line handwritten Chinese character recognition based on crossing line feature. In: Proceedings of the Fourth International Conference on Document Analysis and Recognition, Ulm, Germany, 18–20 August 1997

M. Cheriet, N. Kharma, C.-L. Liu, C.Y. Suen, *Character Recognition Systems: A Guide for Students and Practitioners* (Wiley, NJ, 2007)

J. Dean , S. Ghemawat, MapReduce: simplified data processing on large clusters. In: Proceedings of the 6th conference on symposium on opearting systems design and implementation, USENIX Association, Berkeley, March 31, 2004

J.E. Freund, *Modern Elementary Statistics* (Prentice-Hall, New Jersey, 1984)

S. Furui, Speaker-independent isolated word recognition using dynamic features of speech spectrum. IEEE Trans ASSP **34**(1), 52–59 (1986)

M. Gales, S. Young, The application of hidden Markov models in speech recognition. Foundations and Trends in Signal Processing **1**(3), 195–304 (2007). doi:10.1561/2000000004

Y. Ge, Q. Huo (2002) A comparative study of several modeling approaches for large vocabulary offline recognition of handwritten Chinese characters. In: International Conference on Pattern Recognition, IEEE Computer Society, Quebec, 11–15 August 2002, pp 85–88

H. Jiang, Discriminative training of HMMs for automatic speech recognition: A survey. Comput. Speech Lang. **24**(4), 589–608 (2010)

C.-L. Liu, M. Koga, H. Fujisawa, Lexicon-driven segmentation and recognition of handwritten character strings for Japanese address reading. IEEE Trans. Pattern Anal. Mach. Intell. **24**(11), 1425–1437 (2002)

U.V. Marti, H. Bunke, Use of positional information in sequence alignment for multiple classifier combination. In: International Workshop on Multiple Classifier Systems, Cambridge, England pp 388–398, 2001

M. Mohamed, P. Gader, Handwritten word recognition using segmentationfree hidden Markov modeling and segmentation-based dynamic programming techniques. IEEE. Trans. Pattern. Anal. Mach. Intell. **18**, 548–554 (1996)

S. Natarajan, R. Saleem, E. Prasad, K. MacRostie, Subramanian Multi-lingual offline handwriting recognition using hidden Markov models: a script-independent approach. In: Lecture Notes in Computer Science, 2008, pp 231–250

D. Povey, Discriminative training for large vocabulary speech recognition. PhD thesis, University of Cambridge, 2004

T.H Su, C.L Liu, Improving HMM-based Chinese handwriting recognition using delta features and synthesized string samples. In: International Conference on Frontiers in Handwriting Recognition, 2010

T.-H. Su, T.-W. Zhang, D.-J. Guan, Off-line Recognition of Realistic Chinese Handwriting Using Segmentation-free Strategy. Pattern Recogn. **42**(1), 167–182 (2009)

T-H. Su, T-W. Zhang, H-J. Huang, C-L Liu, Segmentation-free recognizer based on enhanced four plane feature for realistic Chinese handwriting. In: 19th ICPR, 2008

T-H. Su, T-W. Zhang, Z-W. Qiu , D-J. Guan, Gabor-based recognizer for Chinese handwriting from segmentation-free strategy. In: Proceedings of the 12th International Conference on Computer Analysis of Images and Patterns, 2007

A.O. Thomas, A.I. Rusu, V. Govindaraju, Synthetic handwritten CAPTCHAs. Pattern Recogn. **42** (12), 3365–3373 (2009)

T. Varga, Off-line cursive handwriting recognition using synthetic training data. PhD thesis, University of Bern, Bern, 2006

Q-F. Wang, F. Yin, C-L. Liu, Integrating language model in handwritten Chinese text recognition. In: International Conference on Document Analysis and Recognition. 2009, pp 1036–1040

Printed by Publishers' Graphics LLC
DBT130422.11.38.140